Lenny Henry

Who am I, again?

FABER & FABER

First published in 2019
by Faber & Faber Limited
Bloomsbury House
74–77 Great Russell Street
London WC1B 3DA

This export edition published in 2019

Typeset by Ian Bahrami
Printed and bound by CPI Group (UK) Ltd, Croydon, CR0 4YY

The right of Lenny Henry to be identified as author of this work
has been asserted in accordance with Section 77 of the Copyright,
Designs and Patents Act 1988

Graphic novel sequences written by Lenny Henry, illustrated by Mark Buckingham and
lettered by Todd Klein.

We are grateful to the following for permission to reproduce copyright material:

Excerpt from 'Codicil' from *The Poetry of Derek Walcott, 1948–2013* by Derek Walcott,
selected by Glyn Maxwell, published by Faber & Faber, copyright © 2014 by Derek
Walcott. Reproduced with permission from the publisher and Farrar, Straus and Giroux;
Extracts from *Motherland* by Elyse Dodgson, Heinemann, 1984, pp. 5, 17. Reprinted by
permission of Pearson Business; Extracts from *The Oxford Companion to Black British
History* by David Dabydeen, Oxford University Press, copyright © 2007. Reproduced
with permission of the Licensor through PLSclear; Lyrics from 'Sweet Jamaica' written
by Aldwin Roberts, performed by Lord Lebby, The Jamaican Calypsonians, copyright
© 1955. Reproduced by kind permission of Kernal Roberts and family; and an extract
from *The Problem of Pain* by C.S. Lewis, copyright © C.S. Lewis Pte Ltd, 1940. Reproduced with permission.

A CIP record for this book
is available from the British Library

ISBN 978–0–571–34260–0

MIX
Paper from
responsible sources
FSC
www.fsc.org   FSC® C020471

10 9 8 7 6 5 4 3 2 1

For Mama

To change your language
you must change your life.

Derek Walcott

Contents

Preface   ix

1 Mama, Papa and Early Childhood   1
2 The Magnificent Seven   25
3 The H'Integration Project   45
4 The Origins of My Comedy   77
5 Entering Showbiz   117
6 Minstrelsy   145
7 Growing Up Fast   183
8 *Tiswas*   215

Afterword   241
Notes to a Young Comic   243
Acknowledgements   273

Preface

Now, 2019...

I'm in the back of a black cab heading from Westminster, going past Victoria Station. Rain-slicked scaffolding, *Hamilton* the musical, fast-food joints, commuters and an onslaught of targeted advertising that beggars belief. London's brilliant.

I thought I'd attempt a bit of context before we dive head-first into my story. The first thing to say is that this is only part of my story – the early years. To create a memoir from where I am now would involve a massive amount of memory mining. I didn't keep a diary when I was a child, so assistance from the past is not particularly forthcoming.

In many respects I was a normal kid – I loved playing and pretending. There were TV programmes called things like *The Saint* and *The Champions* and *Man in a Suitcase*, and I loved them all. When I walked to school in the morning, I was Simon Templar or Amos Burke or John Steed. These guys didn't look anything like me, but I wanted to be like them. In art classes, when I made a self-portrait of me as a secret agent or a kick-ass cop with super-powers, I invariably drew myself as a white guy, in a sharp suit and sporting a pointy quiff. That was my experience of what was on television all the time. Black people were usually the baddies or the trusty friend with a twinkle in his eye or the victim. I chose not to emulate those guys. I only wanted to be the cool-talking, martini-drinking, gun-toting hero – who was usually white.

This was the early 1960s, so there were very few people of

colour on TV. If we were ever spoken about on screen, it would usually be as the butt of a comedian's joke. More often than not, we were a punchline. But as I reached my early teens in the early 1970s, things were beginning to change.

In the meantime, I'm still in the cab, thinking about the way things were back then.

In terms of this book, I thought it would be worth talking a little about my siblings – my fantastic brothers and sisters, Hylton, Seymour, Kay, Sharon and Paul – because they are a route to my mother, Winnie, who passed away in 1998. I'm also going to talk a lot about my three most prominent friends during my post-pubescent, most formative period: Greg, Mac and Tom. We called ourselves the Grazebrook Crew, after the road where Mac lived, and they remain a key part of my story.

I'm going to discuss growing up and puberty and school and getting up on stage at the Queen Mary Ballroom (a dance venue at the top of Dudley Zoo. The animals watched us go in sober and come out drunk). I intend to talk about as much of my life as I feel can fit into this framework, which I reckon stretches from 1958 to 1980-ish. That takes us up to a crucial point in my development, and includes the first angry outbursts of punk and the related uprising of alternative comedy. Perhaps another book will take in marriage and *Chef!* and later versions of *The Lenny Henry Show* and Hollywood and the like. But right now, I want to focus on this quite tight time frame. It feels manageable.

I've been communicating with my friends and family about the whole writing/memory-mining process. They all wanted to have their say, and I have referred to them when I thought it apposite. I do have a problem with dredging up old thoughts and memories, however. I find that sometimes things weren't how you actually remembered them. You think it sort of happened like that, but there's bound to be a bit you don't quite remember; there'll be the crystalline and honed dinner-party version of that story. But then there's the crushing moment when your mum or uncle or sister or mate tells you, 'It wasn't *quite* like that,' or 'You didn't *exactly* say that' . . . and on and on and on. We reframe and re-edit our pasts: exam results change, our teachers become kinder or more ogre-ish, our sporting prowess more Olympian and our sexual exploits exhaustingly naughty, horny and relentless.

There's another reason for not entirely spilling my internal organs onto the page: there are some things about my childhood that I genuinely don't know. The moments I'm not sure of I've tended to leave out like the least-liked Opal Fruit. The idea that memoirs are a time for settling old scores doesn't gain much traction with me either. My gut tells me that if I was too cowardly or hesitant to sort something out at the time, what good would it do to dredge up the moment again and cross-examine it in retrospect? When I do discuss things or events where I felt hard done by or misused, I hope I've dealt with them fairly.

In *On Writing*, Stephen King compares Mary Karr's evocation of her childhood – as 'an almost unbroken panorama' – with his sense of recall, which appears like 'a fogged-out landscape from which occasional memories appear like isolated trees'. I know what King means here: for some of us, memories are sketched, ghostly things – unreliable. The one phantom thread running through the forest of my story is 'Who am I?' or 'Who should I be for the people around me?' Who do they *expect* me to be? Son? Pal? Comedian? And so each time a new Lenny was needed, I jumped.

For the most part, then, this book is not an autobiography, but a biography. Because I'm writing about someone I used to know.

Nelson Mandela once said, 'Forget the past.' In many respects I think he was right. The past can appear to be this other country, this exalted place where you spent so much time and where so many things happened that were good or bad or painful, and it's difficult to let go, but in the living of life there is forward movement and so you wind up letting go anyway, just by virtue of putting one foot after the other.

So while I'm relatively happy to look back, right now I'm in a cab moving forward and, when I reach where I'm going, I will continue putting one foot in front of the other – and then I'll jump.

I

Mama, Papa and Early Childhood

MAMA

Before anything else, I remember Mama. She was the Jamaican Wonder Woman. I'm being a bit facetious – there were lots of women like my mama. She was of a particular stock, the kind of person who had worked very hard from a very young age. She had powerful hands, and if you were swiped or punched by either of them, you knew about it.

Mama's feet were large. As a child, I would try on her shoes. They were huge – massive boats with heels and a buckle at the front. I would slide around in them pretending to be important, because, whether she wanted the title or not, Mama was the alpha in our family. Papa was tough and 'manly' in appearance, but at home it was very clear who was in charge. Mama was just better equipped for the trials and tribulations of raising a large family in a semi-hostile environment.

Her legs were incredibly powerful. She had obviously spent many years walking the highways and byways of the Jamaican countryside. As a subsistence farmer and market trader she spent hour upon hour working in the fields and carrying straw baskets of fruit and veg to and from the market. Having seen some of these fields, highways and byways for myself, it's clear that walking long distances was the norm for people like Mama and Papa. I now understand why walking was such a big part of her life here in the UK, where she would clock up miles trudging around Dudley and beyond.

Everyone in Dudley seemed to know my mama. As a small child, out with Mama on an apparently endless Saturday shopping trip (when else would she have the time to shop? She was a working woman!), I would note the countless familiar nods from Caribbean men and women. Mama spent most Saturdays going up and down Dudley High Street nodding at every black person she saw. She had a relatively plain face. The experience of growing up in rural Jamaica, working in fields and performing back-breaking tasks for little money, obviously affected her habitual demeanour. She smiled rarely, but when she did, it was fantastic. Most days she wore a mask of granite that said, 'Don't mess with me. I'm Winifred Henry, and if you try anything funny, I'll knock you through a brick wall.' Because she could.

Saying that, she laughed a lot, but mainly in the confines of the house. She was a gifted storyteller, charming, funny, with a great sense of description, outrage and mispronunciations: she didn't say 'certificate', she said 'cer-fi-tick-et'; she didn't say 'film', she said 'flim'. Like a lot of Caribbean people, she would watch her favourite soaps – *Crossroads* and *Coronation Street* – and commentate throughout. Of *Coronation Street*'s resident lothario Len Fairclough:

'Yu see yu? Yu favour dog.'

Of busybody Hilda Ogden, also from *Corrie*:

'What a way she nosey-ee?'

Because I spent a lot of my childhood being disciplined by this woman – with belts, branches, boots, sometimes the occasional pan lid – seeing her laugh was a revelation. All that anger and worry would disappear from her face, and this other Mama would appear – huge smile, sparkling eyes, honking laugh, which I would often satirise, for my own comedy purposes, later on in my career. I loved *this* Mama; I wasn't so keen on the other one – she was too vexed.

Just before Mama died in 1998, she cleverly set me and my siblings a challenge. She was in her pomp, safely ensconced in her bungalow near Brierley Hill. We were all there, in various stages of distress. Mama looked at us and said, 'Humph . . . I bet when I'm gone you'll scatter to the four corners of the earth and never see each other again.' So, when she finally passed away, we vowed that we would meet up at least four times a year.

And that's pretty much what we do, sitting and talking about the things we love to talk about:

– *Mama's cooking; her burnt Christmas cake.*
– *Her way of laughing at things, which came in three stages: a very high-pitched, plosive 'Ha hiiiii', then a 'Woy!' and perhaps a knee slap, and then, finally, as if she'd just remembered she needed to put a punctuation mark on the whole thing, 'Jesus Christ!' (This was before her born-again days, obviously.)*
– *The way she'd crunch ice from a bowl as she watched telly (that'd be in the summer), or the way she'd snack on Scotch bonnet peppers (one of the hottest chili peppers in existence – think molten lava, and then double it). There'd be no hint of pain as she ate, whereas I remember eating a Scotch bonnet fragment by mistake and having to spend the rest of the evening upside down under the cold tap.*

We talk about the way Mama was, who she was, her unshakeable Christian faith in her later years, what she achieved in her time on this earth and what we all learnt from her, because remembering and reflecting on the struggles of the previous generation equips future generations with the wisdom and coping tools that they, in turn, can pass on to their children.

Mama's story begins in Jamaica.

The West Indian migration to Britain in the 1950's was part of a history of migration from the Caribbean islands which had started over one hundred years before. It began with the migration of former slaves, very soon after emancipation in 1834. As free men and women many soon discovered that there was little opportunity and hardly any fertile land left for them to develop. One of the means of overcoming poverty was to leave their island altogether – to migrate. Migration was also thought to be a form of protest whereby former slaves could demonstrate their hatred of a system that had tied them for so long to one place.

(FROM *Motherland* BY ELYSE DODGSON)

Throughout this memoir, I will plump more for my feelings than for accuracy. Knowing my mother's stories so well, research might feel redundant when compared to the actual heart-felt reasons for my mother's actions.

Before I was born, Mama had four children by her husband, Winston Jervis Henry: Hylton, Bev, Seymour and Kay. She also lost three other children – one stillborn and two mis-carriages – before producing Kay, her fourth surviving child. I didn't find out the truth about the dead babies until I was making a documentary retracing my family's roots in Jamaica. My brother Seymour took me to our village and, first, showed me the family home, which was basically two broken-down walls amid a plethora of overgrown greenery. Then we drove down the road to Grandma's house, behind which we found a group of family graves, among which were three tiny, cigar-shaped gravestones.

My papa was thirteen years older than Mama and, to my eyes anyway, a hardened stoic. He probably thought that they'd just go on pushing a plough and having kids and hardly eating. My mama had other ideas. So did her brother, Clifton.

* * *

It was Uncle Clifton's fault. I can see him now: a spiv's moustache, a trilby, which he always wore perched on the back of his head, and a sheepskin car coat. He had made the great leap to the United Kingdom first, to test the waters. He found a place to live in Dudley, in the Black Country, and got a job at Bean's Industries, a company that supplied components to the car industry – anything from crank cases to gearboxes. They were based in Tipton, which is a cough and a spit from Dudley. Clifton worked there for a while and then realised two things:

(a) he missed his family, particularly his sister Winnie;

(b) he needed a wife.

So he wrote to my mother and told her of the great advantages to be had by moving to the UK. You could earn thirty shillings a week, and there were all kinds of factories in which to do so. Hadn't Enoch Powell, a British Tory minister, come to Jamaica and invited West Indian nurses to pack their bags and find jobs in the UK? The dream of a better life.

I imagine Clifton's letter went something like this:

Dear Winnie,

It is I, your brother Clifton, writing to you from the Black Country.

It would be good if you could come here. There are plenty, plenty jobs here, and you could get one easy. Women can earn as much as 30 shillings a week, and I'm sure you'd be able to do other things to make up your weekly allowance.

I know you're tired of breaking your back to feed all them kids back in JA. Tell Winston to get off his arse and bring everybody to England as soon as possible.

It cold here but them have job! Come soon.

Your loving brother

Clifton

P.S. Bring me a wife.

By all accounts, this tempting invitation went down like a cup of ice-cold sick. My father, Winston, had already forbidden my mother from embarking on a life-changing journey to the southern states of America. Some black American preachers had seen my mother testify in church and they'd told her that she should go to America because she could make good money preaching at the tent shows and on the gospel circuit. Mama wanted to go, to leave Jamaica and seek her fame and fortune, but Winston put his foot down. No way was any wife of his going to pack a bag and jump on an airplane to God knows where in the southern states, where they had Jim Crow and all kinds of segregation. And what? Was she expecting him to look after the children on his own? He had things to do as well; he was the man of the family and he wasn't going to allow her to wander off into the sunset. I'm putting words in his mouth, but I can imagine his disdain for this short-lived dream of hers.

For many years Mama felt that she'd been denied her shot at the good life. When Uncle Clifton's letter arrived, she knew this was her chance to break free from patriarchal, poverty-stricken life in rural Jamaica, an opportunity to prove she was someone who could do something significant for her family. She wouldn't take no for an answer, so she saved up money from her work at the market and eventually squirrelled away enough for a ticket and subsistence once she arrived in the UK.

The crossing was £75 or thereabouts, so assembling that kind of dough was no mean feat. And I bet my papa moaned about using that money to catch a hold of some silly dream. But she did it, despite his disapproval. She also managed to find Clifton a prospective wife: Madge, someone she knew, whether via the church or just from around the way. Arrangements were made and Mama embarked on her life-changing journey, accompanied by a very excited Madge. She left Papa, my elder brothers

(FROM Motherland BY ELYSE DODGSON)

Hylton and Seymour and my big sisters Bev and Kay and got on that boat, her and Madge. She was ready to go.

Elyse Dodgson's *Motherland* describes how aspiring immigrants went about leaving their homes, family and children:

'I sent Sharon to the shop to get a cake and when she came back I was gone.'

'I was very sad leaving my kids behind. But y'know, since I had that plan to send for them, I knew it wouldn't be long before I see them again.'

*'I wasn't at all worried or upset because we have always lived in
the extended family. I merely lived with my grandmother. I wasn't
worried or upset. I just got a bit fed up with my grandmother.'*

Once I'd read these words, I contacted my sister Bev and
asked her how she'd felt when Mama left. She replied:
'I was 15 when Mom got on that ship; I felt the separation
and cried.'
I sent the same request to Seymour. His reply was typically
Seymour:
'Len dats a long time ago. What/how we felt is a distant mem-
ory. We were jealous of the guys who had both parents but the
money in letters compensated . . .'
A month later, Mama and Madge arrived in the UK.
Upon arrival in Dudley, there were problems. For a start,
Clifton could only really put up one woman in his flat. Since
Madge had come to marry Clifton, she could discreetly make
sleeping arrangements with him, but Mama had to sleep on the
floor. Mama wasn't pleased about this, but she did it anyway.
She couldn't afford anywhere else at this point.
Though Clifton was as happy as a pig in the proverbial,
Mama's future was less golden. The mother country, with its
promises of open arms, jobs and warm bonhomie, was not quite
as welcoming as Clifton had described. Times had changed since
the arrival of the *Windrush* in 1948. This was now a suspicious
and, at times, bigoted England, one that refused to understand
that the immigrant diaspora had been invited to the UK to make
up for a gap in labour.

*Labour shortages opened up scope for migration from colonial territo-
ries and Commonwealth countries, whose people being British subjects
were, in principle at least, free to live and work in the United Kingdom.
Among this group, workers from the Caribbean, escaping high levels*

of under-employment, showed a particular propensity to take advantage of migration opportunities. Colonial and Commonwealth immigration rates are estimated at up to 10,000 a year from 1948 up to the mid-50's, increasing to over 40,000 by 1957–8, before dropping back to a depression invoked by government deflationary policies to below 30,000 in 1958–9. Caribbean workers demonstrated that they were a useful addition to the UK labour market.

(FROM *Motherland* BY ELYSE DODGSON)

When she first arrived, being out and about was tough for Mama. She often described what it was like to confront racism on a daily basis: she would be followed down the street by children who wanted to know where she was hiding her tail; on the bus, women would feel her face with their hands and ask her whether her skin colour came off; men on the street would make monkey noises at her as she passed; and although she spoke perfectly good English, in almost every shop she entered the staff would speak veeeerrry sloooowllly.

There were signs in the bed-and-breakfast lodgings saying, 'No Blacks, No Irish, No Dogs' – so if you were a black Irish wolfhound you were buggered (© Kim Fuller). It was cold all the time, even when it was meant to be summer, and she never really got used to that. Soon she got sick – it was wintertime in England, when they *had* winters, freezing breezes easing in through the cracks in the windows and underneath the doors, a hoar frost forming on your exposed toes as you tried to snatch a couple of hours' sleep, while your brother lay in bed, cuddled up to his future wife. Mama must have been furious.

She got pneumonia, and it nearly did for her. On the verge of death, she moved out of Clifton's place and found a room in an Indian-owned house that rented out bedsits. These were single-room spaces into which the landlords would cram a bed, a wardrobe, a dressing table, a dining table, some chairs and whatever else could be squeezed in. There'd be a 'gusunder' (Dudley parlance for a chamber pot) stashed under the bed so you could have a slash in the middle of the night.

Which is where Albert Green enters the story. He lived in a bedsit in the same house, and he saw that Mama was unwell and unable to help herself. Albert – or Bertie, as he became known – looked after Winnie through her illness, making her soup, fixing the broken windows, locks and doors. Once she was better he helped her find work at any number of factories and acted as a guide around the Black Country, taking her to pubs and clubs. This relationship would have consequences.

Mama was off and running, earning the money that would get Papa, Hylton, Bev, Seymour and Kay over to the UK. She did it with the sweat from her brow and the strength of her backbone.

PAPA

In 1959 Winston – my papa – arrived in the UK with my big sister, Kay. Papa was a walnut-hard man, dark-skinned, jet-black hair and barely a wrinkle. He rarely smiled or laughed, and when he did, it was usually at some mishap. I remember he laughed loud and long when one of our neighbours slipped on black ice in the street.

Papa was smart as a whip. He spoke occasional Spanish, sometimes out of the blue and for no reason, and smoked Park Drive cigarettes. More importantly, he rarely lashed out and hit any of us. Strong-willed and authoritarian, he would come home from work and demand:

'Turn the TV over, I want to watch the cricket.'

Every night. Even if we were watching the bloody cricket, he'd say:

'Turn the TV over, I want to watch the *other* cricket.'

He could focus on cricket for hours. He tolerated us making

a racket around him and would only occasionally tell us to 'Stop the blasted noise!'

He argued with my mama a fair deal. One of my earliest memories is of sitting in my cot, hands on the bars, and watching him fly across the room at her. And then they'd get on fine; it wasn't *Terry and June*, but they'd be perfectly civil to each other. Papa would hand his wage packet over at the end of each working week; Mama would take it and hand back his spending money. The point is, whatever they would occasionally scrap over, coming to the UK changed their lives for the better, whatever the calypso records said:

> *Many West Indians are sorry now*
> *for they left their countries and don't know how.*
> *Some leave their jobs and their family*
> *and determined to go to London city.*
> *Yes, they are crying now with regret,*
> *No kind of employment now they can get.*
> *The city of London they got to roam*
> *and they can't find their passage to go back home . . .*
>
> ('Sweet Jamaica' BY LORD LEBBY)

Papa would do odd things like wear his pyjamas under his suit. He'd let his nails grow really long (I mean Catweazle long), and he liked a drink from the local pub. Us kids were dispatched there with some loose change from the pocket of his overalls and ordered to buy a jug of stout and to bring back the rest of the money. Kay and I would march up to The Bush, at the top of Blackacre Road, make cute faces at the bar lady and obtain beer and fags for both parents. We'd walk back verrrry carefully with our prizes. You never knew – we might get to keep the change or have a small glass of beer and a smoke ourselves.

My father and I never really bonded. Mama did most of the

child wrangling, and I was also distracted much of the time. I was born in August 1958 and, in many respects, I was a surprise – not least to my mama, who hadn't banked on producing yet another Henry while her husband was still in the Caribbean. Sixty years later, and having been through the complications of relationships myself, I've slowly come to understand the complexities of displacement, loneliness and the need for companionship.

Needless to say, when my father arrived with my big sister Kay (a smidge older than me and very bright), it took a while for him to thaw to the idea of this new kid. But even though it took a godawful long time, he did eventually grow to appreciate me. And throughout my childhood he worked very hard to make sure there was food on the table, clothes on my back and a safe haven for me. He worked *really* hard. He would come home from the factory and at least three times a week he'd go upstairs and run a bath and then lie in it for half an hour. I remember seeing the water after he got out: there was this dark-grey scum sitting atop the surface, with bits in it. I *never, ever* wanted to work in a factory if it made you that grubby after a day's work. But he did it, five days a week for thirty years.

Who Am I #1

I'm about four or five in this black-and-white photo. I love black and white. There's something about it that's more real than colour. It has great power and conveys something much greater than mere verisimilitude. In this picture I'm a pageboy. My sister Kay is a bridesmaid. My brother Hylton is marrying Betty, and my memory explodes whenever I see this photo, because it triggers memories of other weddings that have been buried deep in my subconscious. I'm pretty sure my parents hired me and my sister out as pageboy and bridesmaid for every single West Indian wedding in the Midlands. I know it's wrong to accuse those who are no longer with us, but I'm pretty damn sure they pimped us out for spare change, because when I look at that picture I see a little kid, standing there as if to say,

'When do we get paid?' I look like a professional, like I've got cards printed out and a limo on its way to take me to the next wedding.

I asked Bev about this, and she said that at the time there weren't too many cute brother-and-sister combos, with their own attire, available for all the weddings that were happening in Dudley. So Mama would volunteer us for all sorts of weddings, even those of non-family members.

I look at that kid now. He hadn't really had time to form an outward-facing demeanour. He's just all about being a tiny kid with a part-time job as a pageboy, and he's happy to be anywhere.

VICTORIA TERRACE AND MAMA'S COOKING

After Papa came over, we all went to live in a tiny bedsit on
Himley Road in Dudley. We weren't there for long, though; it
was much too small. With Papa's help, we were able to move to
Victoria Terrace, just up the road, to a huge (to my eyes anyway) house that could hold many more kids and family members. There were three bedrooms on the second floor, one on
the first floor (probably a repurposed sitting room), while the
attic had a teeny bedroom and a larger one. The order of sibling
arrival ran thus: Kay arrived with Papa in 1959, then Hylton
rocked up in early 1960; shortly afterwards, my big sister Bev
and her beau, Charles, made the journey; and the following year
Seymour eased in, seventeen, cool and groovy. They all made
this little Dudley-born kid feel welcome.

It was an old house with an outside toilet. My memory tells
me we had to bathe in a tin bath by the fire, and that a passage-
way was built later to enable the family to use the toilet without having to brave the elements. There were loads of rooms,
which were much in need. The combination of Mama, Papa, us
lot and Bev's growing family all under one roof meant chaos,
confusion and, at times, conflict. There were arguments, complete with shouting and proper fisticuffs, like on the TV, when
Simon Templar would hit the bad guy on the jaw and you'd
hear, 'POW!' and then he'd go flying across the room. That's
the kind of fighting Mama and Papa did. But when it was over,
they'd be fine and we'd all stop the noise and get on with our
lives. There was also a big out-of-tune piano on the landing
and music everywhere, plus the constant aroma of Jamaican
cooking, with all its various components: chili peppers, Scotch
bonnet peppers, garlic, thyme, pimento . . . mmmmm. Mama
was an amazing all-round cook, a specialist in that normalised

15

working-class genre that we love and revere called Mama's Cooking. She had that ability to return from work and create magical meals from whatever was lying around.

We'd be back from school and sat there in the living room – Paul, Sharon and me – watching kids' TV. As soon as Mama walked in, we would hear, at full volume and all in one breath, this unvarying list of our shortcomings:

'But stop! Lard Jesus Chris', ef *yu* see my trial. Yu mean to say, mi haffe wuk every hour the Lard give, from six o'clock inna mornin'? Slave like a daag all day, mek one an' two poun', if mi lucky! An' I wuk in this house, wit' mi two sore foot bottom . . . an' *yu* miz-a-rabble pickney couldn't even peel one an' two likkle potato, soak the rice, mek t'ree dozen dumplin', season the chicken, sweep out the front room, mop the kitchen floor, ketch fire in the back room, re-tile the bathroom, plaster the facing wall in the lounge [etc.].'

This was *every* night.

She was right, of course. We'd come home, watch telly, do bits of homework, poke each other with sticks, naturally assuming that at some point before the news came on, a magical someone would make our dinner for us (by the way, it was always 'dinner', never 'tea'). When I started going to my white friends' houses, they would ask me if I wanted to have 'tea' with them, and I was amazed when their parents would bring out egg and chips and crisps and bits of ham or cheese and a mug of tea. The penny dropped: tea's a meal, not just a drink! This is brilliant! And because their portions were almost always starter-sized, I knew I could go to my house afterwards and have a more Jamaican-sized dinner. This usually occurred at six o'clock and involved a large piece of fried or roasted meat, dumplings (boiled or fried), potatoes (ditto), rice and peas (or sometimes just rice), and something green (we laughed in the face of greens). There'd usually be a chemical-tasting orange/raspberry squash concoction too. This meal would be served on the everyday crockery, the patterns faded and with noticeable cracks, the slightest tap of the fork threatening to snap your platter in two. The food was always piled high, high, high on your plate, like a towering, savoury version of Carmen Miranda's headdress.

We always ate as a family in those days, everyone round the table. In the winter there'd be an almighty fight for who got to sit nearest the fire. We lived in a large-ish but cold and draughty house, so whoever got to sit by the fire had pride of place. However, the consequences were dire because as the heat rose and the room became more and more toasty, rivers of sweat would begin to pour from every orifice, soaking shirt, pants and bum crack. If I'd landed the seat by the fire, I'd soon have to begin the tedious process of bartering with my sister in the hope of changing position.

Me: 'Kay? I'll give you this tasty piece of meat and this piece of yam if you agree to swap places . . .'

Kay: 'You mad? NO.'

The food was almost always delicious. Mama had truly mastered stick-to-the-ribs food and knew how to make supplies stretch. Even though it was just the six of us, she always cooked for twenty-seven people – *minimum*.

When we came home from school and stared listlessly into the cupboards, we'd see geriatric tinned pilchards, asthmatic bags of rice and odd damp scraps of green *somethings* near the back. When Mama looked into that same cupboard, she would see the makings of a glorious feast. We always ate well, no matter how much Mama complained that there was no money. And she complained a lot about that. But still, she would conjure Caribbean banquets for less than a pittance.

When she was older, I would visit her, and whenever I did, I'd always catch her watching daytime TV. Ainsley Harriott or somebody would be in the process of teaching a useless student

WHO AM I, AGAIN?

how to make a nutritious meal for under £5. And Mama would laugh, saying, 'Five poun'? Yu could feed a multitude of people with that!'

I regret that I never learnt to cook under my mama's tutelage. I was too busy getting up on stage and performing whenever I could. From the age of fourteen that was my life. My brother Paul became a really good cook because, as he escaped puberty's iron grip, he was able to watch everything that Mama did, while I was at the Skylight Club in Workington, attempting to figure out why they weren't laughing at the old Frank Carson joke:

I said to the landlady, 'I found a dead flea in my bed.' She said, 'One dead flea won't kill you.' I said, 'I know, but 10,000 came to the funeral!'

Paul was at home learning how to prep salt fish so that it flaked perfectly on the fork; or how to steam rice and peas so that they didn't stick; or the gargantuan task of preparing Saturday soup from scratch, which seemed to involve simmering half a sheep for three days. These were my mother's culinary masterpieces, but my early departure from home and hearth robbed me of the opportunity to actually learn how to make them for myself.

Mama's generous meal-making meant that we were all natural-born trenchermen who treated mealtimes as communal gatherings, full of love, laughter and wisecracks. It wasn't just normal everyday meals at which Mama excelled – she could bake too! Whenever there was a wedding or christening, or just before Easter and Christmas, Mama would receive requests from the four corners of Dudley:

'Miss Winnie, I beg yu mek mi a cake.'

And as long as they paid a little for the ingredients and her time, Mama would undertake this confectionery challenge. In

18

the lead-up to Christmas, our house smelt like a cross between a Caribbean cake shop and a distillery. There were all kinds of dodgy, arcane twirlings, swirlings and curlings taking place in our cellar, with the odd maniacal cackle thrown in for detail.

Mama began cake preparation for the Christmas season months and months before. Ingredients were bought in bulk and stored for what seemed like ages. Then, as autumn's blush took hold of Buffery Park's greenery, we'd notice that the giant mixers would begin their whirrings and stirrings – all weekend long – as the mixtures were assembled: not just butter, eggs, sugar and flour, but a plethora of raisins, glacé cherries, sultanas, berries, brown sugar, white sugar, biracial sugar.

Mama never seemed to measure anything. I never saw her clutching her forehead and screaming at a cookbook, 'Why won't you just say precisely how many half-tablespoons of vanilla, Delia?!' Mama didn't do that. She used the time-honoured Jamaican baking technique of 'dash in'. She'd take ingredients by the pinch or handful and simply dash them into the mixing bowl. She never measured the amount of alcohol; she'd just upend the bottle, let it glug a couple of times, pour herself a small glass, slug that, and then continue.

Mama cooked like a skilled improvisational lead guitarist: she knew all the chords and scales, the flats and sharps, etc., but she could extemporise and make up her own recipes. In the way that Jimi Hendrix could play variations on a theme, Mama did the same with cakes; she didn't need someone else's formula. And then she'd batch-cook, three or four cakes at a time. The aromas drove us giddy, our nostrils mesmerised by the sensational smells emanating from the oven. People we hadn't seen for years would suddenly show up at the house:

'A'right, Winnie, remember me? I teef your car in 1965.'

Mama: 'Is what yu wan'?'

'Yu bakin' cake? It smell good, mi can have a piece?'

Mama: 'Yu wan' mi call police 'pon yu?'

'Call them, yes, but forward me a piece a cake in the meantime.'

I think it was something to do with the alcoholic concoctions that went into the mixture: sherry, white and dark rum, Wincarnis (whatever that is), Ovaltine, cough linctus and the rest. Everything went in there, and whatever she added made it smell even better, more alluring, almost orgasmic.

When I got a bit older – sixteen, maybe seventeen – on Christmas Eve I'd get in from wherever I'd been, on my way to wherever I was going. I'd have my night all planned out, but my intentions would always be swayed by the heroic, mouth-watering fragrances oozing from the kitchen. Mama and my big sister Bev would be stationed amid dozens of sausage rolls and mince pies, Mama elbow-deep in a turkey, prepping it for the uncertain hell known as the 'overnight roast'.

Our Christmas cake would already be in the oven. By now, Bev and Mama would have partaken of some sherry and be sharing stories of Christmases past. Yuletide hits would play non-stop on the radio, like Eartha Kitt's stunning version of 'Santa Baby' (the line about the platinum mine always cracked Mama up). And as the stories grew longer and the sherry-drinking became more brazen, a large, undulating mass of cloud, dark in colour, would slowly envelop the entire kitchen.

The cake is burning. THE CAKE IS BURNING!

Mama would look up, point with her turkey-encased fist and say something like, 'Hmmm, hmmm, look 'pon the h'oven nuh?'

And we'd all look at what can only be described as a 'blouse and skirt, raatid inferno!' Mama would rush over and open the white-hot oven door (no gloves – Jamaican mums are hard), the flames belching from within. Despite this inferno, she'd kick the oven door aside and retrieve the now blackened husk of a cake.

This wasn't the first time this had happened. Bev's expression told the story – yet another Christmas cake incinerated. But Mama would have the whole thing under control. The next stage was *not* to dump the charred remains in the bin; instead, Mama would fetch a very sharp knife and proceed with her patented debridement treatment, removing the dead cake tissue. Sometimes she would remove as much as an inch of burnt cake skin, and within, at the heart of the tragedy, would be the perfectly cooked remains. The cake would, of course, be a third of its original size, but still, it would be just right.

Once this work of culinary genius had emerged from its smoking chrysalis, Mama and Bev would proceed to decorate it with icing, small silver bells and coloured flowers. It was like a fourteen-course meal in one triangular lump. You couldn't eat too much of it due to the alcohol content: two slices and you'd find yourself wandering around the streets, unaware of your name, the location of your house and your purpose in life.

Chris Tarrant received one of my mama's cakes after the Christmas edition of *Tiswas*. She'd saved up a big one just for him, a special, unburnt one. Mama loved Chris. He'd looked after her when she came on the show as a special guest and really made her feel like one of the *Tiswas* family. He took the cake gratefully, put it on the back seat of his car and drove home.

After twenty minutes of, it must be said, some quite *wobbly* driving, Tarrant realised he was being followed by the local constabulary, who were signalling for him to pull over. Tarrant also realised that he felt ... a bit pissed. He pulled the car to the kerb. The copper was in fits.

'Bloody 'ell, Tarrant, you was all over the road! Do you wanna lift to your house?'

Tarrant opened the window, and what can only be described as a solid fog of what smelt like 100 per cent proof alcohol wafted past and enveloped the police officer's head like a rum-soaked burlap sack. I still don't think they believed his protestations of 'Lenny's mum's cake got me drunk on the way home . . .'

Since Mama passed away in 1998, there's been a series of subtle attempts to usurp her baking supremacy. Bev's cakes are delicious, sweet and alcohol-free; Paul's are almost there; Kay's had a go and they have a good taste to them; and Cousin Nena's attempts are so sodden with alcohol only a brave person would even attempt a slice – one whiff and you're out until *News at Ten*. Trust me.

I once made a recording of Mama discussing her recipes. I thought it would be our family's legacy. However, Mama was getting on a bit by this time, the conversations would ramble, and she would absolutely refuse to reveal *any* of her secrets.

Me: 'So, Mama, how much sugar is it again?'
Mama: 'I don't know, you know – mi jus' dash it in.'
Me: 'Yeah, I know you do, fair play to you, but is it one or two cups of sugar?'
Mama: 'It depen'.'
Me: 'Depends on what?'
Mama: 'It depen' on how much cake you wan' to mek.'
Me: (a leetle frustrated) 'OK, so what about the raisins and cherries and sultanas and that?'
Mama: (drifting off slightly) 'Jus' dash in whatever you wan'.'
Me: 'So . . . you don't actually know exactly how much you put in?'
Mama: 'Mi nevah measure nutten, yu know? Mi jus' dash it in, and the Lard will provide.'

Unfortunately, the recording continues in this vein for quite some time, and then Mama falls asleep. Finally, you hear me going 'Rarghhh' and jumping out of a nearby window.

The point is, my mama could really make a cake.

BEING A LITTLE JAMAICAN KID

Imagine Victoria Terrace. It wasn't a council house, but it wasn't a mansion either. It was a big multi-roomed place, chock full of our noisy extended family. It wasn't perfect: it seemed rickety and in need of constant repair. It smelt of cooked-down chicken and Saturday soup and cakes and carbolic. There always seemed to be music booming from the large radiogram: Prince Buster, Elvis Presley, the Beatles, Chuck Berry . . . This was our house, in the middle of our street . . . well, number 4 to be exact, just off the main road, a short distance from the zoo and very close to Rita's corner shop. We lived and thrived and argued and laughed a great deal here.

As a teeny tiny child, I remember being portable, with everybody's face way up in mine and saying things like:

'Look 'pon the chile, him cute-ee?'

'Him favour yu, yu know, Mrs Henry.'

'What a way, him big! Him big, him big, him big so til.'

I grew up in a Jamaican household where everyone spoke in the Jamaican dialect. There were these explosions of Caribbean noise:

'Unnu put the something down!'

'Wha' wrong wid yu, yu finger's bruk? Go fetch yu own water!'

'Mama! Len put di hot peppa in me mout' an' it a bun mi!'

And Jamaican swearing is horrible. Something I really feared were the words that rang out whenever Mama and Papa were angry. Papa would stub his toe, and I'd hear:

'AH WHA' DE BUMBO CLART!'

Mama would burn her finger on the stove, and it'd be:

'RAAS HOLE!'

And when the arguments kicked off, these phrases were grouped together and spat out in staccato fashion:

'Oh, me? Yu tink seh *me* care what yu tink to bumbo hole? Well, tek yu raas clart backside an' garn den.'

'Is me yu a talk to, woman – if I tek my bumbo clart han' to yu.'

'Gwarn den nuh? If yu tink seh yu raas clart bad, pick up yu fis' an' try beat me. I will kill yu two time before yu even re-a-lise yu dead!'

And then one of them would add an 'Ahoa!' at the end just to make sure everyone knew where they stood punctuation-wise.

This was normal to us. And the swearing wasn't even that bad once translated:

'raas clart' was toilet paper;

'bumbo clart' was toilet paper too;

'bumbo hole' was your anus;

'raas hole' was also your anus;

'pussy clart' was a sanitary towel;

'pussy hole' was your front bottom, if you were in possession of such a thing.

When these words were mixed up with old-fashioned Anglo-Saxon, you had a linguistic party. One incredibly brilliant Jamaican derivation from a British swear word was 'fuckery'. It described a mess, a terrible situation, a cock-up: 'Wha' kinda raas clart fuckery is dis?'

There wasn't much cursing in our house, but when there was, it was rarely with a Dudley accent. Jamaican was the norm, and to all intents and purposes I was a little Caribbean kid, eating Jamaican food, listening to Jamaican conversation or arguments, watching my brothers and sisters and nephews and nieces behave in singularly Jamaican fashion. It was (mostly) heaven.

2

The Magnificent Seven

These are my siblings: (left to right, back row) Paul, Hylton,
Seymour, me; (front row) Kay, Mama, Bev, Sharon.
  Hylton, Bev, Seymour and Kay – Jamaica-born, in that order;
me, Paul and Sharon – British-born, in that order.

HYLTON

Eighteen years older than me, my big brother Hylton was an
adult when I was born. I never saw Mama or Papa say to him,
'Go to your room.' In his younger days, he always fought

anyone who bullied Bev or Seymour. He had a powerful sense of justice.

I was a pageboy at his wedding, when he married Betty. They put me in charge of the ring. I was five and I had my brother's gold wedding ring in a box. I'm not sure why he trusted me. When I look at the group photo from that wedding, I can see myself standing at the edge of the picture looking bewildered – who are all these people? Hylton's at the centre of the picture with Betty. They both look like Jamaican royalty. Hylton's smiling, like Sidney Poitier's younger, better-looking, more charismatic brother. He was tall – six foot seven – the Jamaican BFG, long and maaga (skinny). Mama called him Sunny because his smile was so spectacular. When I was little, he seemed so tall I thought Mama had named him after the hotel.

I remember Hylton making a regal appearance at my infant school's open day, when I was about six. I had taken the letter home and had said to Mama, 'Mama, there's an open day for mums and dads to come and find out how we're all getting on.' This is what I heard in response: (*Mama sucks teeth*) 'Open day? How dem mean "open day" . . . of course it's open. If the place not open, that mean I have to take Len to work with me.'

Jamaican mamas and papas go to work; they don't follow their children to school unless something's wrong. So the open-day thing wasn't going to work. My parents were not going to come to my infant school to watch us play with Lego and stickle bricks.

A week goes by and the open day comes. About an hour into it we're playing and drawing and the Lego's out and no one knows what to do with the stickle bricks, and then suddenly the door opens and Hylton walks in, tall and handsome in his church clothes. He has to bend down to get in through the door. There's chaos! The other kids see him, run and hide – they've never seen an elongated Jamaican person at the school before.

But I was proud, because here was this lovely person who looked like me. He'd come to visit me, only for half an hour, but he showed us how to use the stickle bricks and the Lego, and he charmed everybody with that smile. He was always kind to me when I was growing up. I don't remember him ever being angry or saying something mean.

Hylton was a real presence at all our sibling gatherings and always wanted to talk about Jamaica and growing up. We'd get a map and he'd point out places: where they went to school or played or got beaten up, or a particularly fine ganja tree, huge like an oak. Jamaica is beautiful, God is good, the tree was bless.

He had a stroke when he was seventy-one, and it changed him. But the more debilitated Hylton became, the more peaceful and calmer he was. He'd decided to become a Christian once more and his faith brought him great comfort in his final years.

The first time I went to see him in hospital, I was told he was in a certain room on the second floor, so I went up there – didn't ask or anything, just nosed around until I found the room. I went in. He was covered up and his familiar grey head was facing away from me. So I put my hand on his shoulder and said, 'H.'

He turned around, and it wasn't Hylton. It was some other man whose head was the same shape as my brother's! When I did find Hylton, he laughed his head off when he heard what had happened: 'We all look the bloody same to you.'

Near the end, he lost the power of speech and we had to communicate with looks and hand signals – thumbs up for good, thumbs down for bad. Whenever I saw him, no matter how much pain he was suffering, there was never a thumbs down. The last time I saw him, his eyes were alive and sparkling. He didn't have his teeth in, but he still looked handsome. Eventually, I had to go, so I told him, 'I'm off now, Hylton. I love you.' In response he gave me a wobbly yet triumphant double thumbs-up.

I will always remember him as I knew him best: tall and hand-some and smiling. He had a big laugh – really big if something was really funny. He'd come and see my shows, and even if I was terrible, he'd be laughing up a storm.

Hylton loved his kids, loved his grandkids. All of them. He was predeceased by some of them, and although he never artic-ulated his innermost feelings, you could tell he would never be the same again.

He was always kind to me, and I miss him terribly.

KAY

Kay came to the UK in 1959 with my papa. We used to say her name was Kay O'Brien Majority Henry, but it was actually Kay O'Brien Marjorie Henry.

Kay was a huge influence on me due to her impeccable taste in clothes and even better taste in music. She would go clubbing at the weekend, and when she came home she'd have all the latest funk and soul 45s with her. She got me into the Fatback Band – 'Nija Walk', 'Wicky Wacky' and 'Bus Stop' – and tunes like KC and the Sunshine Band's 'Queen of Clubs'.

When Mama wasn't in, Kay played some great music in the front room on our prized radiogram, which was totally forbid-den. She took care of her records too and wouldn't let any of us play them. Of course, when she was out, we were all over them, thumbing them, licking them – just to see if they tasted as good as they sounded. After she'd introduced me to the Fatback Band and their ilk, I began to buy my own tunes at Graduate Records in Dudley. They would package ten non-hit singles together and sell them for 50p, and if you were lucky, one of them might be half decent.

Kay was my hero. Ever since I was at infant school she pro-tected me from bullies and stray dogs. She would just jump into

whatever fray I had managed to find myself in and get involved:
'Leave him alone, he's my brother!'

'You mess with him, you gotta mess with me.'

I had a terrible crush on her best friend, Lorna Wilson, an
Afro-wearing sidekick who accompanied my big sister everywhere. They'd sneak out of the house with impossibly sized
hair, platform boots, hot pants and hippy-style tops. Mama
frowned on this surreptitious behaviour, but Kay knew that if
she approached our mother and said, 'Mama, can I have some
money to go out?' she'd have been laughed out of town.

Kay and I used to get into scraps because I was *always* in her
bedroom. I don't know why. I had my own room, but Kay's was
like an Aladdin's cave, especially when I was eleven and twelve.
She was experiencing stuff in her life that I had no idea about.
Her bedroom was locked most of the time, but when you got in
there, there were so many things: brassieres and tiny rectangular
boxes with strange names . . . I was intrigued and would open all
of these products and lay them out to look at them.

One day Kay caught me in her room, and we had a big fight
that ranged all over the house. We fought a lot and I would often
get the better of her, but once she'd turned sixteen there was
no beating Kay. She was a young woman now, and you'd better not go in her room and mess with her feminine products or
you'd get a beating. During this particular fight, Kay was dealing out punches and kicks like Emma Peel in *The Avengers*.
Unfortunately, I was a twelve-year-old kid on the receiving end
of a major beat-down, wondering when exactly it was going to
stop. But it didn't – she was furious at the invasion of privacy and
wanted to teach me once and for all that I was not welcome in her
room. The battle raged on and eventually took us into the front
room. I fell in, and Kay followed me. There we were on the pristine, super-clean carpet, amid the antimacassars, pictures of Jesus
at the Last Supper, leather sofas and such. On the mantelpiece

was a chalk dog – quite a large item. Kay picked it up and hit me on the elbow with it, right on the funny bone. I began to cry uncontrollably; I thought she'd broken my pointy elbow. It felt like something had given way in there, and Kay was going to pay for what she'd done to me. So I drew on all my powers of concentration, calmed down, stopped crying and waited for Mama to come home. I knew that as soon as Mama found out that Kay had hit me – and not only that, but with one of her best chalk dogs, and not only *that*, but she'd been in the front room when she'd committed this heinous crime – she was toast.

Mama came home, and both of us received the power of her fury. She wanted to know who'd messed up her tidy front room. Who'd chipped the chalk dog? We both got told off in Jamaican, which is hard to take at the best of times. Just for kicks, I could have said, 'This is all down to Kay,' and Kay might have been beaten. But Mama didn't lay a finger on us – she was concerned that I had been genuinely hurt – but she also understood, once Kay had blurted out what I had been doing, why I had been hit repeatedly. She took Kay upstairs and spoke to her, and then came back down and told me not to go in Kay's room any more because 'She's a young woman now, and there are things in there that are none of your business.' I nodded and agreed that I would never go in Kay's room again.

And then did exactly the same thing two days later. I was an idiot.

Eventually, Kay got all growed up and left home. When she got a terrible case of shingles, Mama took care of her, but also told her off for getting so stressed out. We all looked after her then. I was glad to, because Kay had been a non-stop supporter of me at school, had helped with my homework and was my chief protector. I don't think I ever said 'Thank you' (usually too busy bawling), so I'm saying it here. Thank you, Kay. You're the best, most badass sister anyone's ever had.

PAUL

Paul was a great kid growing up. He couldn't sit still or concentrate. The teachers at his school said he couldn't focus and didn't hold out much hope . . . maybe he just needed to be doing something that he wanted to do. He was mischievous, cheeky and funny. Always very funny.

He followed me everywhere. I remember he followed me to school one winter's day and got knocked down by a car on Blackacre Road. He broke his leg and was in a cast for weeks. I felt terribly guilty about that. I think I was doing that 'Leave me alone, what are you following me for?' thing. And suddenly – BAM!

He would follow me and my pals Greg and Mac down to this knackered adventure playground we used to frequent. It had blackberries and rhubarb growing wild everywhere. The roundabout was unreliable, and the swings had frayed ropes. The place was a liability, but Paul and my nephew, Glen, would follow us down there, and while we played football with a tiny tennis ball, they screwed around on the see-saw and acted stupid on the swings, spinning them round and round and round at speed until they whizzed off like dervishes.

Paul loved this game, and stood nearby as a white boy named Gaz Butcher played havoc with the swings. Now, I'm gonna give Gaz some credit and say that he didn't mean to let the swing go with all its weight towards Paul in the way that it did. It was an accident. The swing seat whooshed towards Paul's unsuspecting face – WHAM! – hitting him in the mouth, and although no teeth were lost, he was badly cut around the lips. There was some laughter; it might have been nervous, but there was laughter all the same.

I was really pissed off. I felt that no one was looking out for me and my family. Was this racism? I didn't know. I just walked my little brother home, and although he'd been badly cut, he didn't moan about it or blame anyone or point the finger once. He said he'd been in an accident and had come home 'with Len' because he wanted to rest.

Later on, when he was in his early teens, Paul became a bit of a ragamuffin, hanging out in the park, playing cards, smoking, doing all sorts. He was on Mama's mind a lot, wearing out her nerves. But Paul was relentless. Whatever Mama did or said, he just kept on misbehaving and getting into trouble at school. No one thought to check him for ADHD or whatever; he was just assumed to be 'not that bright' and was allowed to go missing without too much fuss. It was a shame. I knew Paul to be as smart as paint, a quick-witted boy with a sharp sense of humour. He knew his music too, and he could dance. In the early days of hip hop he was in a dance troupe called Spectrum and could be found busting B-boy moves in rehearsal rooms, as well as on stage at the local disco. Spectrum were featured in a TV show called *SWANK* on Channel 4 in its early days.

In the meantime, Paul's highly developed sense of humour – and, for that matter, my sister Sharon's – came to my aid at various times. They watched everything I did on TV and made comments when they saw me:

'That wasn't very good, chap. You had no energy.'

'Who wrote that rubbish? You were a bit joke-light.'

'I don't know how you've got the nerve to come round here after what you did on *Seaside Special* last night.'

And so on. They were ruthless but nearly always right. Whenever I thought I'd just about got away with something substandard, Paul and Sharon would appear and teach me that I had, in fact, *not* got away with it, and for an hour or so they would show me, with diagrams and re-enactments, why a particular routine hadn't worked.

My proudest moment involved Paul. In the 1990s I was

curating a writers' retreat called A Step Forward. My production company, Crucial Films, had managed to squeeze some money from the BBC in order to host a three-day writers' workshop for black, Asian and minority ethnic (working-class) writers. We had read dozens of scripts and managed to narrow the applicants down to thirty or so. I then invited people such as the BBC's Head of Light Entertainment, James Moir, producers John Lloyd and Charlie Hanson, and writers Richard Curtis, Anne Caulfield and James Hendrie to come down and give lectures on writing sketch comedy, show films, hold one-on-one sessions and judge a writing competition. Paul had written some sketches for our perusal and had been chosen for inclusion.

We had six groups, and each one had to write a number of sketches and then swap work with another group and be judged. We had asked some comedy actors to come down and perform some of the sketches. We would find out who'd written what later.

A sketch about John Barnes – about him being such a good football player that he not only dominated defence but also midfield and front-field; that he was able to get off with girls during play, cook gourmet food and build an extension to very high standards – was hilarious. Victor Romero Evans (of *No Problem* fame) performed the John Barnes super-fan with a Jamaican accent and a sense of high dudgeon. We all laughed so much; every single development of the premise got bigger and better laughs. There was an explosion of appreciative applause.

The writer's name was announced: Paul Bevan Henry. I almost burst with pride. My baby brother had proved that he could sit down, write and create something worthwhile; it just had to be something that he really wanted to do. He went on to write on *The Real McCoy* and *The Lenny Henry Show* (1984–8, produced and directed by Geoff Posner). As a writer, Paul is

WHO AM I, AGAIN?

such good fun in the room. He can make you laugh tears of joy at a funeral. I've seen him do it – he's *that* funny.

He can cook 'big food' too, churning out plate after plate of proper Caribbean food, like dumplin', rice and chicken, cook-down beef, ackee and salt fish, and every ting as well. I'm deeply jealous of this. As someone who had to use someone else's hands for the chopping sequences in *Chef!*, it pains me to say my brother Paul can do all that stuff standing on his head.

We should see each other more than we do. I intend to fix that . . .

SHARON

Sharon was visiting Mama's old village in Clarendon, and an ancient lady wrapped in several layers despite the heat, head covered with a scarlet cloth, carrying a gnarled stick, looked at Sharon and told her she 'mus' be Winnie Henry child' because 'yu have her frame'.

Sharon's the baby of the family, and she was adorable from the off. She was pretty much Paul's female junior sidekick. They were always mentioned as a pair – Eric and Ernie, Cannon and Ball, Sharon and Paul.

Sharon is real smart, and makes friends easily. After Papa died and she grew into her teens, I became more of a father figure in some respects to both her and Paul, which was weird considering Seymour and Hylton were older than me. I guess this was because after winning *New Faces* in 1975 I'd become the de facto breadwinner. But I didn't mind; in fact, I loved it. Even when I came home one day to find them playing frisbee with my albums, hurling them through the air at assorted wildlife in Buffery Park: the Ohio Players (*whizz, smash*), Miles Davis (*whizz, smash*), *This Is Soul: A Stax Compilation* (*whizz, smash*), Peters and Lee (actually I didn't mind that one being frisbeed).

Sharon was on the back of the bike when I hit a bump in the road and went flying over the handlebars. She'd have been about six, and apart from shock she was fine, but I managed to slide along the road's gravelly surface on my face for several yards, removing the top layer of skin on the right-hand side. Until my skin grew back, after three months or so, I looked like the Jordan Peele alternate casting for Two-Face in the African American version of *Batman*. But Sharon was fine.

I don't remember her being in any trouble at school, and I don't think she ever got into trouble at home. It was sickening. There was us getting 'nuff bitch licks day and night, and there was Sharon deftly sidestepping it all with a butter-wouldn't-melt smile on her face.

Sharon is bloody funny too, quick-witted, sharp – she's got the jerk-saucy banter. She and Paul are still a double act to this day, and when they get together they can make me laugh like a drain, almost at the flick of switch. Not necessarily jokes per se, although one-liners do abound; it's usually more a mash-up of Dudley-speak, Jamaican sayings, imitations of family and hugely overinflated opinions (add alcohol to this and it can get crazy like a mofo). Sharon has her own theatrical management business. She actually looks after people in the business. Actors, writers, things like that. She's amazing. I'm so proud of her. Why the hell won't she represent me?

SEYMOUR

In 2018 Seymour and I went to Jamaica to make *The Commonwealth Kid*, a BBC documentary about post-colonial Jamaica and the surrounding areas. We visited where he grew up and where Mama and Papa used to work. It's a place called Concord, in the Claremont district, near Bensonton, in St Ann Parish.

We drove to where my elder brothers and sisters went to

school. They used to run there every day, carrying a piece of breadfruit or yam and, if they were lucky, a piece of chicken. When they arrived, a grown-up would relieve them of their burden and promise to cook it in time for lunch. If they were even a minute late, they got one or two lashes with the cane. Jamaican school don't play.

There are photos of Seymour hanging out near Grandma's house. He's smoking a roll-up and there are several young people – some with dreadlocks, some with tight curls in lines – sitting with him and smoking too. In all the pictures Seymour looks calm, assured and relaxed. And that's as it should be. Whenever I've spoken about him on stage or television, the person I describe is always tall, lean, handsome and militant, the kind of guy who doesn't take shit from anybody, but doesn't bang on about it either.

Seymour was born in Jamaica, and he was the last of the siblings to come to the UK. Apparently, he didn't speak until he was four. When I asked him why, his reply was classic Seymour: 'There wasn't anything to say.' Mama said that once he started talking, he wouldn't bloody stop. Apparently, he was a Professor of Naughtiness: he had a PhD in Mischief, and wreaked havoc throughout St Ann Parish. He was always fighting and sometimes he'd be beaten badly by kids from a rival town. Shortly before she passed away, Mama told me that she had to get on a donkey, ride to a nearby village and yell at the top of her voice, to anybody that could hear, 'Anybody in dis raatid hole place wan' mess wi' my son should know that when they do that, they're messin' wi' me as well.' When she saw that no one from the village was about to challenge her, she would spur the donkey with her heels and ride out of town like John Wayne in an apron.

Seymour had to take his fair share of licks growing up, but he revealed to me during the filming of *The Commonwealth Kid* that when he arrived in England to find three-year-old me, it was as if all his Christmases had come at once – something which he'd never said to me before. I was blown away by that. Truth be told, he and I pretty much always got on. He was a legend in our house. Mama had ruled over us all with an iron fist and the threat of multiple whacks with a broomstick/iron cord/shoe heel/clenched fist. However, for Seymour, it all stopped when he caught Mama's fist mid-punch and just held it there, until she backed down and told him to get out. Seymour left immediately and joined the RAF, vowing never to return. But Mama was there on his passing out day, weeping with pride as he marched past in his dress blues.

Seymour was a very good son, and wherever he was stationed, he would come home bearing gifts from that location – vases, rugs, sculpted heads, cups, saucers. Mama loved everything and made a big fuss of him whenever her prodigal son strolled in from abroad.

Because Seymour lived with us for a while, his bedroom was there for us to explore whenever he wasn't home. As a kid I loved going into his room. There was all sorts there: weird 'educational' magazines under the bed, heavy boots and a sizeable collection of vinyl that had to be seen to be believed, with lots of Stax and Atlantic – Wilson Pickett, Otis Redding, Carla Thomas, Aretha Franklin, Booker T. and the M.G.'s – and plenty of reggae. It was a cornucopia of musical delight, and whenever I could I'd sneak in there, borrow an album, then creep into the front room (*verboten* to pickneys) and play said record quietly, experimenting with dance moves while trying not to break the special china.

Seymour caught me in his room a couple of times, which is why I have two army boot-shaped dents in my skull. He could throw a boot with unerring accuracy could Seymour. He was a Jamaican ninja.

When Seymour left the RAF, he did a variety of things – fixing TVs, electronics, early computers, all sorts. I grew closer to

37

him when I made my first foray into show business and moved down to London. When I lived in Wembley, Seymour was in Harlesden. I found myself spending more time with him and learning a great deal about him and my family. It was a more equal relationship than it had been before. We'd go clubbing to Gulliver's in Mayfair, drink and eat together. Seymour came to gigs and hung out, and he always had an opinion about the show. In many ways I think he was disappointed when I disappeared down the Black and White Minstrels rabbit hole: 'You? Performin' in a minstrel show? I mean, what the forkin' hell yu do *that* for?' We tend not to talk about it these days.

My experience with him on *The Commonwealth Kid* brought us even closer together. Standing on the site where your parents lived years and years ago, or indeed looking at the graves of three deceased siblings, are events that can bring anyone closer together. I also felt an absence, having never experienced Jamaica in the same way as my elder siblings.

Seymour used to drive a bus in London, and one of the things I'm proudest of is that on the day of the 7/7 bombings in 2005, he ferried frightened and injured passengers away from the chaos to safety. He doesn't talk about this much, but even to this day you can tell the whole experience had an effect on him.

Seymour is always a disruptive presence during our sibling soirées. He's usually there with a glass of brandy, his flat cap and his rapidly disappearing teeth, talking about home and his memories of how things used to be. I was most moved by him at Hylton's funeral, when I realised just how close they had been. Seymour began the eulogy and was so upset he stopped and couldn't finish. There was a pause, he looked down at his feet and tears dripped from his eyes. Then it was as if all the sibs watching had the same idea simultaneously: we all walked purposefully towards the stage and hugged him until he was able to finish his speech.

Seymour has three children – Prima, Stuart and Simone – and he also has grandchildren. I tease him endlessly about this, because he doesn't behave like a granddad.

BEV

Beverly Parker is my eldest sister. She came over to the UK from Jamaica in November 1960 (when I was two), and soon after married Charles Parker from Laws Hill, Concord district, Jamaica. They quickly produced three boys. Charles went to work in a factory, while Bev mostly stayed at home and took care of the house and the kids.

By this point we had moved from Victoria Terrace to Douglas Road. The house was at the end of a long terrace, two storeys high, with a barely perceptible hairline crack down its front aspect. It was built on top of a septic tank that would burst its seams each rainy season, leaving us to wade through an entire street's waste, until the local water board came and fixed whatever was wrong.

The house had a medium-sized kitchen, a front room (as mentioned earlier, Jamaican rules clearly state that children are NOT ALLOWED, UNDER PAIN OF DEATH, to go in the front room), a back room and a living room. There was a shared toilet and bathroom on the upstairs landing. The décor was typical Mama: lots of flock wallpaper, lino, bits of carpet (bought with bingo money), pictures of Jesus and an eclectic collection of second-hand furniture. We had a lilac tree in the front yard, and Papa had a vegetable patch near where Mama used to park the car. There was an alleyway to the left of the building that led to the back entrances of the neighbouring houses.

I remember the house being packed with Henrys and Parkers just about getting along. Bev's three boys – Trevor, Mike and

Kenneth – were all born in the early 1960s, and so were very close to me in age. We all slept in the same bed, four similar-sized kids sharing the space. It wasn't great. We took it in turns to wet the bed. There were many times when I dreamt I was asleep in a submarine that had just been torpedoed. Tough times.

Bev was a pivotal figure in my life because Mama was at work all the time. She'd leave the house before 7 a.m. most mornings, leaving Bev in charge for the rest of the day. Bev had her own children to deal with, so to a large extent she would lay off us younger siblings. She was a cooler, non-violent version of Mama. As long as we did what was asked, we were allowed to go about our business without fear of being hit with a Dutch pot upside the head. Bev used to calm Mama down, stop her acting rashly. A good influence.

Bev and her family eventually moved out – too much conflict and overcrowding. I was sad to see her go, though I was glad to get the bedroom to myself. I could put pictures on the wall. I didn't have to divide up the chest of drawers and the wardrobe any more. I could put my books down without fear of them being torn up or thrown away by a malevolent nephew.

Bev and Charles now lived a ten-minute walk from us, in rented accommodation nearer to Dudley town centre. I missed Bev's calming presence, though, especially after one particularly alarming experience. I was nine years old or thereabouts. Somehow, the sap was rising, and I was very interested in the opposite sex. I was captivated by the photographs of naked women doing the ironing (from *Health & Efficiency* magazine) that we found over in the park. Why were they doing the ironing naked? Why were the whole family naked as they ate their breakfast? Why were these torn-out pictures of semi-clad females abandoned in the bushes? It was a Pandora's box of questions.

I liked reading too, and when Seymour left two large crates of paperbacks in the cellar, I was over the moon. I would creep downstairs into the murky, dusty world of the Henry cellar, where there were old record players; overstuffed, dead armchairs; bits of abandoned timber with long, lethal, rusty nails sticking out; old clothes and shoes; and the odd bit of costume jewellery. I loved being down there, and during the holidays when everyone was out of the house at work or play, I would sneak in and have a good old root round.

Seymour's collection included a considerable number of westerns, which all had semi-clad bar-room queens or glamorous Mexican ladies with low-cut blouses on the front; there were war books, with femmes fatales in tight army uniforms; there were spy books, of the James Bond variety, all of them with suggestive covers featuring 007 in a tuxedo, crisp white shirt and bow tie, his Walther PPK held aloft, and usually with a naked woman draped around him.

I'd go down to the cellar to look for the sauciest cover, one with the barest flesh on show. I was in heaven, though I didn't quite know how to take it any further. For the time being, I was content just to stare at the covers, read a bit of the text and dream of kissing a Mexican bar owner in a low-cut frock. I'd be in my school clothes. To impress her, I'd doff my cap. Maybe she'd help me with my homework? My imagination ran wild.

I did this on a regular basis: wait for everyone to leave the house, hop, skip and jump down to the cellar, rummage around in Seymour's crates and find a book with the prerequisite semi-clad figure on the cover.

One week we had a power cut and the lights went out, so I had to improvise. I did what I'd seen someone on TV do – made a torch by putting paraffin in a milk bottle, using some newspaper as a stopper. Then I tipped the bottle upside down to soak the paper with paraffin, set light to it and read by torchlight. As someone later pointed out to me, 'Len, you were *actually* reading by Molotov cocktail!'

I was having the time of my young life down there, reading about spies and sexy double agents whose clothes fell off at just the right moment. I was completely enthralled reading about their exploits, but I must have left the kitchen door open because there was a slamming noise upstairs, and as I jumped in surprise the torch fell into the crate of dry books, and with a huge WHOOF! it was aflame!

This was all in the space of nanoseconds. One minute I'm James Bond, the next I'm the boy with no eyebrows. What was I going to do? The flames were licking the ceiling of the cellar, as though it was the tastiest lolly on earth. I was in serious trouble, no idea what to do. I ran upstairs to get some water to put the fire out. I came back down and threw a tiny pot of lukewarm water onto the crate. SSSSSSSSSSS! The water disappeared into steam!

I ran upstairs to get a bigger pot of water, but by the time I got back down the flames had travelled from one crate to the next. WHOOF! And now they were dancing around the cellar, feasting on all the other dry bits and pieces of tinder lying around. Shit. I was in such trouble.

I left the house and ran for three minutes up Blackacre Road, then crossed over and went into the phone box to call the fire brigade. We didn't have a phone at home, so when I got there I looked at the dial with all its complicated numbers and finger holes and didn't know what to do. A very kind elderly person saw me shriek, 'IT AY FAIR!' at the top of my lungs and showed me how to dial 999. The fire brigade were on their way. I'd left the back door to the kitchen open so that they'd know where the fire was. It turned out there was no need to do that. As I approached the house I saw dark grey smoke billowing out of the window, like it was the back window of Snoop Dogg's Escalade – the fire brigade would immediately know which house was ours. As I got closer I got a better look at the house. Yup – still on fire. I burst into tears and ran away.

I found myself at Bev's house. She allowed me in, and I stayed at hers for the rest of the day. I made small talk, I helped her with the kids, I played with Mike and Kenneth and Trevor as though nothing was wrong. But deep down, I knew that (a) I'd burnt the house down, and (b) when Mama came home from work, I would be toast.

Bev was very kind. I hadn't told her anything was wrong, but she'd guessed. She knew I was scared of Mama single-handedly picking up the car and dropping it repeatedly on my head. Eventually, she said, 'Maybe you should go home now? It's getting dark.'

I didn't want to go home. 'Can't I stay here . . . till I'm twenty-five?'

Bev was insistent and pushed me out of the house. I walked as slowly as I could, dreading the beating that was inevitably about to happen.

I once got a letter from a black journalist who wanted to take issue with me about the stand-up I'd done about getting beaten by my mama. He said it trivialised physical child abuse, turned it into light entertainment, didn't help us to grow and move past a stereotype of Third World parenting. I agree with all that, but the problem is, I grew up with beatings and clartings and bitch licks. It might be a trope, but it was true. My mama was brutal when she disciplined us. She once hit me in the face with a frying pan. She threw a chair at me. And, of course, she could punch you and knock you through a brick wall. I was so frightened on that walk back to what I was now calling 'the ruins' that I was literally shaking.

When I reached home, I was relieved to find that the house was still standing. The fire had been extinguished with a minimum of fuss and mess. The firemen had done their job brilliantly, cleaned up after themselves and gone on their way.

Mama was waiting in the front room. It looked like she had been crying. I prepared myself for the beating of all beatings. What would she hit me with now? I quaked in my boots and stood in the doorway, waiting for everything to be bounced off my head.

Mama took one look at me and said, 'Go to y'bed,' in a soft, resigned voice. So that's what I did. I went to bed – and I spent the next four hours sleeping with one eye open, knowing that at any minute she'd sneak in through the bedroom door and start lashing my backside. But she didn't, and I woke up the next day exhausted but relieved.

I think that Bev might have had something to do with my not being beaten. Although the cellar had been gutted by fire, the house had remained intact. Apart from an odour of burnt paperbacks, there was no real damage. What good would it have done to beat a child senseless because of an accident? I was lucky, I guess. Mama had thought long and hard about what my fate should be and decided that to hit me would only exacerbate things. She knew that if she'd reacted in the way that she normally did, I might not survive, and she couldn't cope with that. So she controlled her traditional response and took another view. I'm convinced that my self-imposed mini-exile at Bev's helped Mama to meditate on her future actions.

3
The H'Integration Project

ASSIMILATION

Mama lined us all up in the hall. I might have been six or seven. I remember our terrible flock wallpaper, peeling at the edges, odd patches of damp everywhere, the smell of last night's oxtail stew wafting through from the kitchen and Mama in her work clothes towering over us. She looked serious.

Who Am I #2

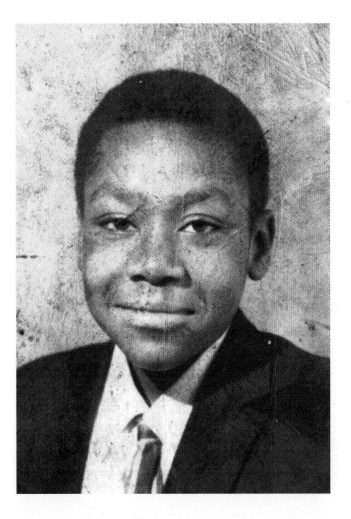

*I'm about eight or nine. We couldn't afford the school tie, so
I'm wearing something that in Mama's brain is the closest
thing. My hair's combed and I'm kind of half smiling as I look
at the camera. It's not arch or cheeky or attitudinal; it's bland,
as if I don't know what sort of face to put on in this situation, as*

if there were things I could tell you about my life at this point, but I don't want to bother you with them. I'm not going to give away all the sweeties from my jar just yet. So right now I'm just going to sit here, have my school picture taken and split, 'cos I want to go out and play. And they tell me I'll never leave here if I don't have this picture taken.

I remember being shy, not particularly argumentative. There was no one-upmanship or 'getting the last word in' or 'imposing my will' where my mama was concerned. At this age, and pretty much until I was eighteen, it was best to agree with everything she said, because if you didn't, the consequences involved hospital food. So here I am. I don't want to get hurt and I don't want to hurt anybody. So I wear my face like this and hope no one notices.

AT SCHOOL

By their very presence in schools, black children also threatened to undermine the education of white children, as teachers were forced to divert essential time, skills and resources away from white children to meet the linguistic and cultural needs of black children. Hence, black children's race and cultural differences came to be defined as the problem, rather than the shortcomings of a system unprepared and unable to respond positively to their needs and aspirations.

Funds were made available under Section 11 of the local government act 1966 to enable teachers to provide black children with the skills that would facilitate their 'successful' assimilation into British society.

(DAVID DABYDEEN, JOHN GILMORE AND CECILY JONES (EDS), *The Oxford Companion to Black British History*, P. 138)

I think at the beginning my attempts at integration were thwarted by overenthusiasm. Also, when you're one of three kids of colour in the entire school, they tend to lump you together. At Jesson's junior school, Michael Colman and I were the only black kids in our year. We used to fight each other just for company. I drifted a bit at Jesson's. I can't remember what I learnt there, but I do remember reading almost the entirety of Charles Dickens's canon. Memory's a strange thing. I can remember fighting Michael and reading *Little Dorrit*, but I can't for the life of me remember anything useful that was taught in those classes. Thankfully, just before the eleven-plus we moved to a new house, going from Dudley central up to Buffery Park. It wasn't particularly far – about a mile or so – but the demographic changed considerably. Now I was attending St John's primary school, where there were many more black and brown kids to contend with. At first I was afraid that I might get lost among them all, but it worked out in the end.

St John's was a rough place, with oversubscribed classrooms, a tiny playground and very few resources. Strangely, I remember it as being a relatively happy experience. There was some racism and a bit of bullying, but you came to expect that in those days. If someone pushed you, you shoved back. The big event at St John's was the eleven-plus exam, which sifted the proverbial wheat from the chaff by determining who would go to the grammar school and who would not. We would not only be answering questions on the actual curriculum, but also tested on our verbal and non-verbal reasoning, yet I don't remember any preparation for this exam. It was a fiendish IQ test as much as anything else, and we were not forewarned at all. My friend Greg Stokes tells me that at Kate's Hill primary, the kids were sat down and told about the eleven-plus exam the previous year, and then, pretty much every week, given past papers to study. I'm still pissed off about this; it's probably the reason I took up further education later in life. I just wanted to prove to myself that I wasn't thick; that I could, given time and fair warning, learn something.

Needless to say, I flunked the exam. Even though Seymour had waved a ten-bob note in my face and said, 'If you pass the eleven-plus, this is yours,' I failed miserably. I turned the page of the exam sheet and saw non-verbal reasoning questions for the first time in my life and had no idea what I was looking at. A cold sweat engulfed my entire body and I shut down. End of story.

My mama and papa didn't seem too bothered about my failing the eleven-plus – 'You'll work in the factory or something. Nuh bodder yuself wid it.' This was the Midlands, after all, where there were more factories than paving stones. It was more or less expected that an able-bodied boy would end up working in a car factory or labouring somewhere. Tony Foley's dad worked as a scaffolder and throughout his entire school career you'd hear Tony saying, 'I don't have to do this 'cos me dad's a steel erector and I'm gonna work with him.' Getting a job wasn't the problem; the problem was finding a career that you could be proud of. Unless you were lucky enough to go to university, the idea of embarking on a career you might actually enjoy seemed out of the question.

After the eleven-plus debacle, I wound up going to Blue Coat secondary modern on Bean Road, which was a three-minute walk from Douglas Road, near Buffery Park. To get there you had to cross the notoriously tricky Blackacre Road, where my brother Paul had his accident. Blue Coat had formerly been an exclusive Church of England school, housed in very sacred buildings, with a large playground and, I presume, church services at every opportunity. It had been in existence since the sixteenth century; old pictures showed the student body in cap and gown, but the uniform in the early 1970s was blue blazer, grey trousers (pleated skirt for girls) and a blue-and-yellow tie.

Once again, the demographic of the school was mixed, but predominantly white, though there was a healthy mix of Afro-Caribbean and Asian kids. There was the usual racist stuff to contend with. For a brief period I had a fight every single day with a kid who didn't like what I looked like. He would utter, 'Move, coon,' or 'Oi, nig-nog,' or whatever as I walked through the school gates. Now one thing everybody knows about me is that I cannot fight. If you asked my sister Kay whether I can handle myself in a scrap, she would throw back her head and cackle like a witch. I was hopeless. Every day I'd be rolling around on the ground with this kid who hated me because I was black. After a while I got tired of this constant scrapping and tried to think of a way out. The particular escape route I chose would lay the foundation for my future career.

I walked in through the school gates, this kid said his usual, 'Hey, darky/nig-nog/coon,' and put his fists up, and I said something like:

'Not this again. Ya must really fancy me, 'cos you're always tryin' to get me to roll around on the ground with ya.'

Him: 'Shut y'mouth, coon.'

Me: 'Here we go. You hit me, I hit you, we fall on the ground and hug. Why don't we go and have dinner and a movie first? Cut out all the fighting?'

Him: 'Are we gonna fight or wha'?'

Me: 'You could buy me a ring – mek it official?'

What I've missed out is the glorious bit. Whenever we had our arguments at the school gates, other kids would gather in a circle and yell, 'FIGHT, FIGHT, FIGHT!' until they either lost their voices or the altercation had finished. This time these kids actually laughed at what I was saying. And even though the kid gave me one and two pops upside the head, the laughter made me feel immune. I kept on making the funnies even as he continued to kick and punch. Eventually, someone in the crowd said, 'Jesus, leave him alone, man.' The rest of the crowd joined in, and soon my attacker simply stopped and walked away. Sure, there were other times when I was racially abused or attacked for no reason, but I had a handle on what to do now. I had a weapon – humour. Result.

By the time I was twelve or thirteen, I'd had an epiphany. I knew I could make people laugh with the things I said, but now I was doing something else: I'd begun to impersonate voices, people, things all the time. Humour would be my armour. This really helped with the H'Integration Project too, because if you can make people laugh, you're breaking down barriers – and I really needed to break them down at Blue Coat secondary modern. Girls ignored you, teachers belittled you – it was no picnic. Even our headmaster admitted that Blue Coat was a 'school on a racist sink estate'. So I needed all the help I could get. Luckily, this was a boom time for people like me who wanted to entertain their friends. The TV output in the UK in the late 1960s and early '70's was perfect for kids like me. Every teatime there were cartoons such as *Top Cat, The Flintstones, Atom Ant, Tom and Jerry, Bugs Bunny, Daffy Duck, Porky Pig, Huckleberry Hound* and *Deputy Dawg*. There were great programmes on in the evening too, and if you begged and whined enough, you might even be allowed to stay up and watch them: *Burke's Law, The Prisoner, The Champions, The Saint, Thunderbirds, Stingray, Captain Scarlet, The Avengers, Doctor Who, The Tomorrow People, The Man from U.N.C.L.E.* and many more.

I watched all these and absorbed the way people moved, talked and cracked wise. I imitated gun shots and explosions and rocket blasters. I watched Mike Yarwood, the premier impressionist at the time. He could do almost anyone – Harold Wilson, Tony Hancock, Frank Spencer, Steptoe and Son, Denis Healey, Edward Heath. I watched him and copied every intonation, every grimace, every eyebrow-raise. Yarwood learnt his voices by taping radio and TV programmes and mimicking the voices fastidiously. I learnt them by copying what he did.

I also watched *Who Do You Do?* on London Weekend Television, a much more raucous and cheaper version of the Mike Yarwood set-up. A group of impressionists from clubland would dress up as various characters and tell jokes or engage in repartee. Peter Goodwright and Paul Melba shone here. There were a lot of impressionists on the scene – maybe this was something I could do? I stole jokes from every light entertainment show I could watch, whether it was *Opportunity Knocks* with Hughie Green or *Sunday Night at the London Palladium* or *The Comedians*. The latter was my favourite because it was basically one comic after another telling jokes to an unseen audience. This high-rating programme made stars of people like George Roper, Ken Goodwin, Stevie Faye, Colin Crompton and Bernard Manning. Goodwin's jokes suited my schoolboy style:

I was walking down the street – settle down now – and I saw this bloke with a dog that was wearing brown boots. I said, 'Why's your dog wearing brown boots?' He said, 'His black ones are at the mender's!'

I was a fan of Stevie Faye:

This docker's left the dock gates and he's doin' 40 miles an hour and the dock policeman's chasin' him, and he's neck and neck, and then – wham! – he rugby tackles him.
The policeman says, 'What you runnin' for?'
The docker says, 'I was timin' yer for tomorrer!'

So as my body exploded with acne and hormones, I began to develop an arsenal of voices and ideas and jokes that would stand me in good stead for the next thirty years.

The Comedians also boasted a triumvirate of black performers: Charlie Williams, Jos White and Sammy Thomas. These three were an enormous influence on me, simply because I'd never seen black comedians on TV before. I'd seen films on TV in which African Americans looned around and popped their eyes while playing servants and maids and crazy-legged dancers, but I'd never seen a black guy in a suit telling jokes. In the US they'd already experienced Bill Cosby, Richard Pryor, Flip Wilson, Nipsey Russell and many more, but the demographic is different in the States and they also had the Chitlin' Circuit, where black comics could ply their craft and earn a crust. Eventually, mainstream TV would come knocking once they'd established themselves.

In the UK we had the working men's clubs, which were usually affiliated to a factory, a local coal mine or a textile mill. You worked all week and then spent your hard-earnt cash at your local working men's club. These places usually had entertainment in the form of a guitar vocalist, an organist and singer, or a comedian/compère. They also hosted mid-priced talent from all over the country. This is where everyone learnt their trade, including comics like Sammy, Charlie and Jos. Charlie had been a coal miner and had played football for Doncaster Rovers. He was as Yorkshire as they come – he just looked Caribbean. Charlie told jokes against himself in order to get the audience on his side. At the time, that was the way forward. I imagine if a black comic came on stage in the late 1960s/early '70s and embarked on a set about Malcolm X and Black Power he'd get his ass kicked, so Charlie came on and said, 'If you don't laugh, I'll move in next door to yer – that'll bring your rent down.' He'd also do jokes about growing up poor in Yorkshire and working down the mine: 'We're all t'same colour down t'pit.' Charlie's laugh was infectious; he genuinely looked as though he was having the time of his life.

Here was a minuscule pool of black talent getting regular work on TV, but with no black producers, writers, script editors, directors, etc. – that was the 1970s. There were programmes like *Love Thy Neighbour* and *Till Death Us Do Part* (both written by white men) and *The Fosters* (adapted from the original American scripts of *Good Times* by Jon Watkins, who was also a white sitcom writer), but these were all attempting to address racial issues from the perspective of the dominant culture. Black people were *not* creating programmes for British television or taking clubland by storm.

So I watched and subconsciously took in what the black comics were doing, but the majority of what I learnt came from what mainstream culture had to offer.

THE GRAZEBROOK CONDUIT #1

I count myself in nothing else so happy
As in a soul remembering my good friends.
(WILLIAM SHAKESPEARE, *Richard II*)

This quote encapsulates my relationship with my friends in Dudley. My companions and running mates in my teens and early twenties – Greg Stokes, Martin (Mac) Cooper and Martin (Tom) Thomas – were and are *compadres* of the highest order. Our halcyon time together has passed into personal legend; they made my transition into broader society almost effortless, and I will always be grateful for that.

We don't see each other as often as we used to, but how could that be possible? From 1972 till 1975 we saw each other almost every day, whether we wanted to or not. We were glued together at the hip, forehead and side, good and bad, drunk or sober, funky chicken or the boogaloo. I loved every experience.

My mother's H'Integration Project for the Henry children was in action by the early 1970s. From the age of thirteen onwards my task was to get out there and socialise with white boys of my own age. I still hung out with my black friends, but this was different. This was a mission of the highest order, and pretty soon I was in a gang of sorts. Not gang-banging in a mofo-type gang, but more a 'jumpers for goalposts, Fab ice creams, recording Alan Freeman's Top 40 rundown on a Sunday night, watching *Top of the Pops* and falling in love with Suzi Quatro, eating a pork bap in Dudley on a Saturday morning, going up the Baggies on a Saturday afternoon' type of gang.

My mission, which I fully accepted, was to make friends and hold on to them for dear life. This was a telepathic lightning bolt from my mother every time I left the house. From 1970 onwards, for the duration of every six-week summer holiday I'd be in Buffery Park sifting for companionship gold. There were lots of people to choose from, but Greg, Mac and Tom were the gold standard.

GREG

I met Greg Stokes one overcast day over in Buffery Park and I liked him straight away, mainly because he didn't present as a 'type': he wasn't a skinhead or a greaser. He was normal, tall and floppy-haired, wearing corduroy trousers, boots, a checked shirt and a windbreaker. Greg said hello immediately. His Black Country banter was endless, as he told jokes and stories in a laid-back Dudley drawl. Our friendship was effortless. He was walking his dog, Butch, a collie who was really friendly and non-violent. I was able to crouch and say hello to Butch in a way I never had before.

Often you could be in the park and dudes wouldn't acknowledge you, even if you had been chosen to play on their football team in a pick-up game. If you were black, you had to be thankful for whatever attention white guys gave you. Greg didn't make me feel like that; he made me feel like an equal. Though only fourteen, I was hanging out with someone who was nearly eighteen and had a car! I closed my eyes and jumped into this new friendship. We spent the day throwing sticks for Butch and talking about the world and our place in it.

He lived across the park, near the top of Blackacre Road, just round the corner from The Bush pub, which was very handy for his dad, Doug, a great bloke who liked a pint on occasion. His mum was called Avery, which I always thought was a lovely name. She made me feel welcome whenever I went to their house. She was shy but was incredibly kind and considerate towards not just me, but all of Greg's pals. Greg had a sister, Jill. She was also shy, so we didn't talk much, but she was cool.

Greg's friends were different to the people I knew from my school and from over the park. Quite a few of his grammar school friends seemed older than their years. Some of them had big sideburns or the beginnings of rainforest-like facial hair. Some of them were in a band that Greg dragged me to see in someone's cellar. They were pretty good, sang 'The House of the Rising Sun'. I was jealous that these kids who were only a bit older than me owned musical instruments and their own mode of transport. I was always the only black person in these gatherings, but the sting of being different and standing out would last a mere moment and then I'd just join in with whatever was going on. This wasn't a time for being closed. I had to be open – to fun, laughter, difference and unusual drink combinations.

Jump, Len, JUMP!

Greg was a Bob Dylan, Beatles and Simon & Garfunkel-type guy. We had a wonderful time of listening to things repeatedly in the hope that I would be converted to folk music. I could certainly appreciate it, and I still love Paul Simon both on his own and with the tall curly-headed dude. Of course, I'm a Beatles fan – in our house Kay made sure that the Fab Four were all we listened to for the longest time. She even made me wear a mop on my head and pretend to be Paul McCartney so she could marry me.

This was the start of me developing a broader taste in music. Elvis, Chuck Berry, glam rock, pop, R&B, disco and funk were still uppermost in my musical mind, but over the next few years, because of my yearning to belong and my friends' eclectic tastes, I had to make room for different types of music.

Greg's car was a shocking, eye-wateringly green Austin 1100, which he christened the Lime Green Flyer. Once he had passed his driving test – after mastering the gears and parallel parking in supermarket car parks all over the Midlands – we began to explore beyond the boundaries of our small neighbourhood. We were all drinking in pubs now. I was a not-so-secret underage drinker, while Greg, Mac and Tom loved drinking pints. It was as though they were practising for an adulthood that didn't really exist any more. I wasn't a big fan of the taste of beer, but I craved their company and they were my peers, so I did what they did.

Greg had a big say in where we went. When Mac and Tom had cars, they had an influence too, but in the first instance it was Greg. We went to pubs all over the Midlands. There was a weird yokel-style attitude going on in some of these places. We walked into one pub and there were all these raddled old white dudes inside. Greg went up to the bar to get the drinks in, and I went to check out the jukebox; there then followed a lull, a small silence, during which a man's voice could be heard saying, 'We don't get many of 'um darkies in here . . .'

I turned to see their puzzled eyes taking me in – for them, this was a close encounter of the Jamaican kind. I slid my coin into the slot, played a reggae banger (probably 'Funky Kingston' by Toots and the Maytals) and went back to my seat.

There's a first time for everything, I suppose.

Greg even invited me to go out with him and his first girl-friend. She was a blonde bombshell whose dad owned a pub. Greg had met her at a party and she'd made it clear that she wanted to get together with him. I think Greg may have been a bit nervous because he invited me on their date, which involved going for a drink and then snogging in the car for a bit before he dropped her off at home. I think I was an excellent gooseberry, interjecting only when all the windows steamed up or a crap record came on the radio. I would wipe down the windows and then change stations until something funkier came along, before settling back in my seat and continuing to listen to the radio.

Greg and my other mates would often lend me money. Growing up in a working-class family and not having a Saturday job meant that I was often broke. The pocket money I received every Friday did not extend beyond a bar of chocolate and a can of Coke. I needed much more than that if I was going to go clubbing and drinking with my mates. Greg had a Saturday job at Mr Doughty's corner shop and he was very generous, which meant that when we went out, he would often give me a couple of quid to pay for my admission into the club and to buy a drink or two. Tom and Mac did the same. Their financial assistance meant that I got to go and see places I would never have seen without them.

Greg got cross with me at times about not having money, but never angry enough to break up our friendship. He'd been to my house and understood by osmosis that my family weren't exactly rolling in it. By the time he went to Leicester University, I was already in show business and spending most of my time in London or on the road. There was no way we could continue our friendship in the same mode it had been in when we were in each other's pockets every day for months on end. On the odd occasion when we did meet up, I would feel a fleeting pang of sadness as he regaled me with tales of all the new friends he was making, the new jokes and running gags, and how he was listening to different types of music.

I think we're better now at staying in touch than we were during that first instance of separation, and it's a testament to our bond that we still want to be friends and see each other on occasion. I was very happy to read a poem to the congregation on Greg's wedding day. We're friends because we're friends because we're friends . . . and I'm glad about that.

MAC

Mac – aka Martin Cooper – lived across the park from me, past the substation with the mutant rhubarb and near the posher, more middle-class houses. He lived at the bottom of Grazebrook Road, and when we wanted to give our gang a name, the Grazebrook Crew was Mac's idea.

It took five or six minutes to run down to Mac's house; ten or twelve if you were strolling on a hot day. Mac was tall, handsome, with squinty eyes (he would need glasses later), the inventor of weird dances at the Queen Mary Ballroom: the Chair, the Fly-Fisherman, the Charlie Chaplin and the Shovel were all Mac additions to the dance-move canon. He had a very quick wit, always ready with the fast comebacks, the gags, the smart observations. He was the most 'out there' of us. He liked to argue and loved a drink – I mean, *loved* a drink.

I *adored* going round to Mac's house, especially near Christmas. His mum was a legendary baker and would begin experimenting with pastries and fillings for her Christmas banquets as early as October. She always had sausage rolls and mince pies on the go, and I think I was a favourite of hers because I ate everything that was put in front of me. She'd often say, 'Has Lenny got hollow legs? He hoovered that lot up in a second, didn't he?'

Mac and I got close because for the longest time we only had a black-and-white TV in the Henry household. The Coopers had a big-ass colour TV – it took up half of the living room. I loved going round to their house to watch *Top of the Pops*. Mac's home was a different world to my usual environment: they had central heating, there was a constant flow of snacks and cups of tea – and a running commentary from Mac's dad throughout every episode of *Top of the Pops*. Mr Cooper took issue with any male pop singer who displayed femininity, so performers like T. Rex, David Bowie, the Sweet and the Glitter Band had him apoplectic with rage.

'Is he gonna eat that microphone?'

'Is it a boy or a girl?'

'Has he got a rugby ball down his pants?'

'Military service for the lot of 'em.'

And on and on and on . . .

Mac would tease his dad throughout the programme, and I would laugh in wonder as I noted the cultural differences between my family and his. Mac was allowed free rein in that house; his parents let him do what he wanted most of the time. He cheeked his parents continuously and sat with his feet on the furniture – there was no front room. His was a house of plenty; there was never a sense of need.

In our house Mama had very strict rules about what I could and couldn't do. Proper meals aside, there was no spare food available for snacks, apart from hard dough bread and butter, or maybe some dry bun from the week before. If I cheeked either of my parents, I'd probably find myself in an ambulance, with the paramedics standing over me and saying, 'She hit him with a frying pan? Who does that?'

Mac had everything he wanted, including a record player and a brilliant record collection, mostly based on Radio 1's *John Peel Show* playlist. He introduced me to Emerson, Lake & Palmer (particularly Keith Emerson's bravura rendition of *West Side Story*'s 'America'), Black Sabbath, Led Zeppelin, King Crimson, Ashton, Gardner and Dyke ('Resurrection Shuffle') and much more. Like Greg, he was eager to push the envelope of my musical taste. I wasn't just some kid who only listened to Dennis Alcapone and Toots and the Maytals; I was listening to King Crimson and Yes too. OK, I was hypnotised by the mince pies and sausage rolls, but I *was* taking it all in. This was part of h'integration.

Jump, Len, JUMP!

Mac was a prodigious drinker, which was unfortunate because, like the rest of us, he couldn't really hold his drink. Mac was strictly a two-pint guy. He was very interested in the idea of drinking lots and lots of pints, but if he exceeded his two-pint limit, a different kind of Mac would emerge, and we'd have to deal with the fall-out. The beginning of the pissedness was always fun and involved us trying to impress girls by being silly, doing stupid voices, cracking jokes or using one of Mac's signature dances to pull focus. The Chair and the Fly-Fisherman always drew comment from girls, sometimes even favourable. But post-two-pints Mac could get bolshy, slightly cross-eyed, pugnacious. On noticing the signals, Greg would lean over and hiss out of the side of his mouth, 'Start the car,' and we'd escort Mac from the premises before he was chinned by an irate boy-friend, a bouncer, or both at the same time.

TOM

My most unlikely friendship, perhaps, was with Martin Thomas – although we all called him Tom. I'll try to describe what this relationship was like, but I'll preface my remarks by saying that there were two Toms: Before He Goes into the Navy Tom and Post-Joining the Navy Tom.

I always felt that Tom hadn't quite drunk the Kool-Aid as far as I was concerned. He had to be convinced that this raggedy, no-money-having son of Jamaicans was worth having around. At first he was all angles and attitude, acting tougher than he actually was. I always thought that he was hilarious. He had a baby face; no one believed him when he told them he was eighteen, and he was always being ordered out of pubs for being underage, while I – who looked older than my age – would get served immediately.

He and I used to play-fight, and sometimes it would get rough. Because of my size I would always win, plus I wasn't scared of Tom – he couldn't fight his way out of a paper bag. That would change, though, post-navy. I understood why he had accepted his nickname of Tom: it was more alpha male, made him sound tougher than he actually was.

He also liked the idea of the Grazebrook Crew, but I think he would have preferred it if we'd gone up the football on a Saturday and kicked ass. Whenever we went up the Baggies, Tom always wanted to go round the opposition end and cause trouble, but the rest of us were wimps – 'Nah, you'm alright, Tom. I'm gonna get a pie and a hot Bovril.' We really didn't want any trouble at all.

I couldn't quite believe that this really intelligent guy was such a wannabe hooligan. His mum and dad, Harry and Sylvia, were such nice people; they couldn't have known what was going on, and they wouldn't have countenanced a boot-boy in their midst.

Because I felt (quite wrongly) that Tom wasn't that keen on me when we first met, I used to feel out of place at his house, but after a while he got used to me. We'd go and call for him, bang on his door, and his sister Judith might answer and let us in. There'd always be something good cooking or baking, and we'd all gather in the living room, which was a riot of yellowing stippled walls and corduroy furniture. If we were in the kitchen, we'd be offered biscuits and cups of tea in the good china. Tom's mum, Sylvia, was very middle class, although I didn't know it was called that at the time. She'd been a headmaster's secretary at a local school and did everything just so. If it was teatime, she'd offer cheese on a plate.

CHEESE ON A PLATE

Ingredients
Several thick slices of Cheddar cheese (strong)
4 slices of bacon (cubed)
1 large onion (thin slices)
Salt
Pepper

Method

Lay slices of cheese in a heat-proof Pyrex dish until the surface is covered. Place under a hot grill.

Fry onion until translucent. Add bacon.

Take onion and bacon and add to the cheese in the dish. Add half a cup of full-fat milk.

Let the mixture brown under the grill.

Wait until there is a brown skin on top and the cheese is melted. Add salt and pepper to taste.

Eat with crusty bread. Delicious.

Sylvia was also always having Tupperware parties, so if we rocked up the next day, we'd be given containers of sandwiches or mini-pies or tiny cakes to take with us. I loved going to Tom's house. Sometimes I used to go there when he wasn't around just to hang out with his mum. We'd chat about school and whatever activities I was doing. I'd ask her about her day, and she'd chain-smoke and do whatever she had to do while talking to me. The Thomases had a complete set of the *Encyclopaedia Britannica* and many *Reader's Digest* editions of books I'd never read. Three classic books crammed into one volume – great for when Tom was playing football and I needed somewhere quiet to sit and read.

Tom's dad, Harry, lived and breathed cricket. He would always want to talk to me about great matches he had seen or played in. One of his friends was a black cricketer, about whom he never failed to remind me. They were an incredibly inclusive family, and during the latter stages of my time in Dudley (before I went off to London, after Greg had gone to Leicester and when Mac was off doing management training) I was a regular there, reading, chatting to his parents and hanging out with Tom. Eventually, he joined the Royal Navy at officer level – his O- and A-level exam results had been off the charts. He went off around the world, aged twenty-one, ordering dudes around who were much older than him. I'm not sure that sat very well with Tom, and when he came home on leave, you could tell that the sense of responsibility was wearing him down. He was smoking a lot and being quite grumpy. I made a joke once and tried to initiate play-fighting to get him out of his grumpy mood, and he did one of those weird martial arts things, where all of a sudden my hand was up my back and my face against a wall – like WHAM! I didn't challenge him to a play-fight ever again. The navy had changed him. He had become one of those 'My hands are lethal weapons'-type dudes.

Strangely, after the launch of my showbiz career in 1975 and the sudden influx of work in every corner of the British Isles, Tom and I once again had something in common. We were both misfits, outsiders who, although we were from Dudley and loved it, were now away from home much more than we were there. We had a common frame of reference and could both talk about 'What it was like to be away from home all the time'. Tom would show up in London or Great Yarmouth or Bournemouth just to hang out for a few days. I appreciated that. He was also one of the first people to see my adopted daughter, Billie. Tom did a cool thing: the press had no idea that we'd adopted a small ten-week-old kid, so it was important to keep her relatively concealed for a time. Tom put on a papoose with Billie facing towards him, and we were able to walk a two-mile circuit, giving Billie some fresh air and me the opportunity to walk somewhere with her other than the backyard.

Tom has a big grin on his face in those pictures of us in Blackpool and those taken later at my house of him carrying tiny baby Billie. He lives in Canada now, and although we communicate through Facetime or Skype, as tends to happen it has proven difficult to keep in touch. He's a mensch, though: whatever's going on, if I want to talk about anything – family, showbiz, friends, career path, parenting – Tom will have an unusual take on the situation.

Who Am I #3

*In this picture I'm doing an impersonation of Tommy Cooper.
What's interesting are the expressions on the faces of my
classmates. They had never looked at me like this in my entire
school life. By this time I had been performing at the Queen
Mary for a year, so although my efforts meant I looked like
a black Walter Matthau, inside I was thinking, 'Oh my God,
they like this! They like me! This is brilliant!'* (The Black
Country Album: 50 Years of Events, People
and Places, *Graham Gough, 2012*)

WHO AM I, AGAIN?

GIRLS

I have to talk about girls. Girls intrigued me. In childhood and early adolescence I went to church every Sunday, where there were girls – gorgeous black girls, hair perfectly oiled and straightened, starch-stiffened blouses and sticky-out frocks, fishnet stockings, flat pumps and the merest hint of the reddest lipstick.

These girls tormented you with the way they sang and moved during the hymns, as they gyrated for the Lord, then tossed you the odd devilish smile. They seemed possessed by the heavenly spirit. They would vibrate, weep, jiggle, wiggle and sing with a sense of spiritual enjoyment unmatched by Slade on *Top of the Pops*. But if I asked them for a date, I would get nowhere. They were not interested in me as dating material. I got no play. I was a living, walking, talking joke to these girls.

It's my own fault, I guess. Let's face it, I didn't look like 'boyfriend material'. No one wants to date a no-money-having guy with patches on his trousers. Also, I wasn't tough, I wasn't very good at fighting, and these girls definitely wanted to be with someone who looked like they could protect them.

I'd see them in the week or at night when I was running chores for my mama. They'd be talking to one of dem boys who had recently arrived from back home, the ones who went to the reggae club up by Green Park. They were aged between fourteen and nineteen and wore clothes that made them resemble their fathers: leather waistcoats, tight trousers, heavy shoes and trilbies or pork-pie hats. These guys played dominoes and cursed like their grandparents. Some ran amok in the streets late at night and carried razor-sharp knives for protection.

The church girls wanted a tough guy. It seemed so unfair, but these *were* hard times. The National Front was out there starting trouble if you were walking down the street and had black skin.

Of course, these girls wanted a manly, hard-as-nails, dumplin'-and-rice protector, not some British-born fish-and-chips yout' who didn't know how to fight. When you're being attacked by racist thugs – 'Come on then, nig-nog, what you gonna do?' – you can't just come out with an impression of Kenneth Williams. So I stopped yearning for them. They didn't want me, so I decided that I didn't want them. (This feeling would wax and wane throughout my teens – eventually, I realised it wasn't to do with black girls in particular; it was more to do with my own insecurities and hang-ups. The *second* I got to London, I realised that there were plenty of black and brown girls – fine as wine in the summertime – who would chat and smile and dance with me. Perhaps I was just in the wrong place at the wrong time . . . Dudley in the 1970s. Jump, Len – jump!)

But over in the park, things were different. I made my friends – and any girls who were around – laugh a lot. Sometimes that led to snogging, and that was joyous. Usually, it would be a behind-the-sheds/toilets/big-horse-chestnut-tree kiss, because some of these girls didn't want to be seen kissing me. The kiss would be great, but if anyone walked by, they'd almost tear your bottom lip off trying to get away. I remember kissing a *bi-racial* girl over by the toilets. Mama found out where we'd been kissing and beat me with the broomstick. 'Yu couldn't tek dis nice girl out fe dinner and a movie and den to the Holiday Inn? Why yu don't have no manners?'

Some girls didn't care where you kissed them – the high street, the park, the counter at the local Wimpy, the back row of the pictures, the front seat of the bus. It didn't matter: if they liked you, you got to kiss them whenever and wherever. I was pretty shy – so were most of us – but somehow, during the post-pubescent summer holidays, when our sap was rising (with all that implies), we forgot our reticence and got to kissing. I think this was also a major trigger for my entertainment aspirations:

my showing off in local pubs, clubs and bars drew the attention of girls, and that was a good thing.

Between the ages of nine and fifteen, I had the usual childhood transitions to negotiate. I was growing up. My voice went from Aled Jones to Barry White in the space of a few years. My feet kept growing: at nine, I was a size 9; by twelve, I was a size 12. I was Dudley's Big Foot. Other things were happening too. I became very attracted to members of the opposite sex. I had no idea what this was all about, but I wasn't alone. My friends at school, even at the ages of ten and eleven, were uttering naughty things about our female classmates, and we wondered why our bodies were changing shape at such an alarming rate. One kid in our class had a full-on set of sideburns like Oliver Reed's Bill Sikes by the time he was twelve. Others among us were putting on muscle and experimenting with wispy facial hair. I wasn't one of these guys: I was growing upwards but not outwards and, try as I might, no hair was forthcoming in the facial area. But the merest whiff of a Sir Francis Drake-type goatee was making itself known in my pants area. What the hell was going on there? Why weren't my parents talking about this? Don't they have puberty in Jamaica? During the holidays, whenever I left the house to do God knows what, Mama would look at me, as if to say, 'I'm not gonna say any ting to yu, yu wi' find out soon enough. Jus' mek sure yu come back by dinnertime.'

And there were things going on over at the park that, had she known about them, would have horrified her. There was a lot of snogging, mostly near the end of the day and usually involving cider, a pack of twenty Park Drive and Jeanette from Selbourne Road. This was all very innocent, but all manner of experimentation was happening. It was as if we were out of control, as if it wasn't really us doing it. The physical need to learn about this stuff was the imperative, almost as though we were being manipulated by our sexual urges and need for knowledge. It was as if every time I came within fifty feet of one of my female classmates or one of the girls in the park, my entire body would say, 'Don't worry, Len, we've got this.' And we would be consumed by each other, kissing until it got dark and we had to go home.

There were also weird self-exploratory moments. There was a lot of size-comparing. Several of us boys would secrete ourselves behind a bush, drop our pants and observe. Somebody would always have a ruler and we'd all be measured. I'm pretty sure my data revealed nothing monumental. Once the ruler had dropped, I'd be met with a sad shake of the head, the word 'average' hurled in my face.

Buffery Park was extraordinary. It was where we'd find the remnants of old magazines: odd, yellowing, torn-out pages from *Health & Efficiency*, *Penthouse* or *Playboy*. *Health & Efficiency* was the scariest, its underlying assumption being that nudity was normal and should be treated as such by the general populace. The women and men in the photographs didn't pose seductively or provocatively for the camera; they were always playing netball or volleyball, or painting at an easel. These pictures made us laugh a lot. The more seductive fare of *Penthouse* and *Playboy*, however, aroused odd feelings that had us snaffling the odd page, folding it up, hiding it away and sneaking off home with it.

This was the early 1970s, surely a more innocent time – and yes, there were dodgy people around the park, but we knew them. One weirdo was a guy whom we all called Gerald. He spoke in a pronounced Black Country accent and had a club foot, which didn't stop him chasing after us when we cheeked him. Gerald exposed himself to us on several occasions, and would also regale us with filthy rhymes, most of which began, 'I gorra dog with two dicks.' He seemed to have an endless supply of filth. The key things here are that (a) we recognised him on sight and so could run away if we wanted to; but more

73

importantly, (b) he was ours. We owned him. We could pick him out of a line-up and recognise his voice in the dark. After he was hustled out of the Dudley Odeon for interfering with himself during *Bambi*, we saw him in the park the next day and told him how the movie ended. Community spirit in action.

This journey, like sailing round the world solo, was very much a 'single-handed' affair for the longest of times. The only news you received regarding the outer hinterlands of sexual activity would be from classmates, park mates or the magazine fragments found in the park. This led to a confused growth period during which sex was discussed a lot (usually inaccurately), laughed about (usually cruelly) and eventually experienced (usually disappointedly). I had no idea where to go to get informed about sex. I knew I wanted it, knew I had to have it, but no grown-ups were helping me to navigate these difficult waters. It was just me and a bunch of numpties down the park with no map, fuelled by cider, cigarette smoke and our imaginations. The Jamaican-born boys, particularly the ones who had been born in an agricultural area, were *miles* down the road – they'd seen livestock in action.

Interestingly, the grown-ups had all the information we needed to know; they just chose not to tell us. I started to understand what Big People's Business was. Whenever Jamaican adults were in a room talking in hushed tones, with music on in the background and cigarettes being smoked furiously, we'd always be ushered out of the room and threatened with violence, hearing the words 'Come out ah de room! Big People talkin',' or 'Pickney! This is Big People Business! Tek yu backside an' garn!' I've just turned sixty and I'm only just realising that Big People's conversations are full of the stuff of life – sex, drugs, rock 'n' roll, the whole bit. No wonder they didn't want us to listen.

THE GRAZEBROOK CONDUIT #2 . . .

Time conflates now, it subtracts and bends and twists and leaves gaps. The period between the ages of eleven and fourteen seems to blur, and my memory does not serve me as well as it might. But I do remember me and the lads playing football in Buffery Park, mainly on the patch of grass in front of the green bench where the old-aged pensioners sat. We'd set up the goals (two jumpers, naturally) directly in front of the bench, and if you scored and knocked an old codger off, you got an extra goal added on.

There were adventures to be had in the park: day-long games of hide-and-seek or kick the can, and twenty-a-side (sometimes more) football. We also played vicious cricket matches – us versus recently arrived tough guys from the Caribbean. Freddie Nettleford, who had arrived some years before, would bring these young lads over to the park and challenge us to a game of cricket, and stupidly we would agree. After fifteen minutes of having a leather cricket ball hurled at our heads at eighty miles per hour, we'd cry off and run away. Those guys could bowl fast fast fast. Another source of fun was doing an 'all pile on', where everybody would just lie on top of some unfortunate person in a big heap. I think the record was seventy kids piled on top of this poor kid. I think he had trouble breathing, but he was alright in the end.

At fifteen I was working in the Safari Bar at Dudley Zoo, which was situated within the crumbling walls of Dudley Castle. While the Queen Mary Ballroom was a chairlift ride away at the top of the grounds, the Safari Bar was situated at the lower end.

The zoo had seen better days, even then, but there was still something splendid about it. People thronged around its gates on a bank holiday, and the bars and restaurants made a pretty penny over the summer period. I'd been fortunate to get work at the Safari Bar in the summer of 1973. Greg and Mac already had jobs up at the Queen Mary, and they had put in a good word for me. There was an enormous chef called Robin, an attractive barmaid

75

called Carol and an Irish head barman called Steve. The boss was a skinny Italian guy called Leo, who called me 'Chocolat' and paid me a few quid a day off the books. I loved sneaking off in my spare time and visiting Cuddles the killer whale. I always felt sorry for him somehow. There was a lot of time in between services to have fun and mess around, so that summer and the next I participated in all the high jinks that were to be had, while using any spare time to practise my impressions, voices and jokes.

On New Year's Eve the Grazebrook Crew and I decided to go clubbing in West Bromwich, the Las Vegas of the Midlands. We met in the Safari Bar, which was problematic for me as I'd just been fired by the boss for terminal lateness. I arrived first, wearing my snazzy Freemans catalogue checked jacket, which I was painstakingly paying off at the rate of 15p a week. I clocked myself in the mirror – cooler than cold.

An old colleague of mine was working behind the bar and she hinted that there might be free drinks. She slipped me a lager and lime. Result! The rest of the Grazebrook Crew arrived, eager for their first drinks and dispensing banter about girls, the crapness of some discos, and the rest. I told them I had no money. The lads were pissed off.

'How comes you've never got any money?'

'Why ent y'got y'self another job?'

'We shouldn't have to carry you all the time. Y'gorra pay your own way, chap.'

It was hard to bear, and in many respects they were right. I just got all hot in the face and couldn't come up with an answer. They decided that if I couldn't pay my own way, they'd leave me where I was, so off they went, leaving me at the bar, alone. It was a real lesson for me. I had to figure out how to pay my own way in the future, otherwise I was going to lose my friends. What was I to do?

Thankfully, the Queen Mary Ballroom, just a chairlift ride away, would provide an answer to that problem.

4

The Origins of My Comedy

LEARNING ABOUT JOKES

I had always been obsessed by jokes. Whenever there was a comic on TV, I'd write everything down. I had notebooks full of other people's jokes. A lot of the material was unusable because it was adult. I was a kid, a young teenager.

The only gags that seemed to work for me were the ones I could match to a voice. So for an army joke I'd be Windsor Davies from *It Ain't Half Hot Mum*. *Some Mothers Do 'Ave 'Em*'s Frank Spencer was always looking for jobs, so I could do building site jokes as Frank, doctor jokes too. Because he was an idiot, you could put Frank in any situation and he would be funny.

Basically, I stole from everybody. If I saw something that worked, I took it, building up a routine as an impressionist.

The typical comedian's fodder at the time would go something like this:

Bert and Dave work together. They make a deal that whichever one dies first will contact the living one from the afterlife. So Bert dies. Dave doesn't hear from him for about a year, figures there is no afterlife. Then one day he hears Bert speaking as if from a distance. Dave's over the moon. 'So there is an afterlife! What's it like?' he asks Bert, who replies, 'Well, I sleep very late. I get up, have a big breakfast. Then I have sex, lots of sex. Then I go back to sleep, but I get up for lunch, have a big lunch. Have some more sex, take a nap. Huge dinner. More sex. Go to sleep and wake up the next day.' 'Oh my God,' says Dave. 'So that's what heaven is

WHO AM I, AGAIN?

like?' 'Oh no,' says Bert. 'I'm not in heaven. I'm a bear at Dudley Zoo.'

This type of joke never worked for me because it was a 'story' joke. When you're an impressionist you have to be funny straight away. They laugh at the voice and its accuracy, and then they laugh at the joke. To do an impression of Frank Spencer and then embark on a three-minute joke – probably not a good idea, especially in the clubs. You've got to hit them – Pif! Pif! Paf! – otherwise they start talking or heckling, which means you need shorter jokes: set-up, punchline, bang bang bang, one after the other. The subject matter has to suit the character you're impersonating. Luckily for me, it all came together like light-ning in a bottle for my TV debut. But after that, the remainder of my career was rocky as hell.

If you were black and on TV in the 1970s, you were expected to tell jokes against yourself and maybe do gags about other races. This was all about playing to people's fear, but also disen-gaging any aggro while you were on stage. The reason Charlie Williams self-deprecated in a broad Yorkshire accent was to stop the audience getting their digs in first: ''Ey up, old flower, stop laughin' – ooh, she's cryin'. 'Ey, old love, don't rub your mascara, you'll be darker than me!' Jos White would say, 'I'm browned off, I'm browned off.' I was subconsciously being schooled in what it might take to get over to a predominantly white audience. Rule number one seemed to be: get all the dodgy racist jokes in before they did.

But I didn't begin like that. I had no plan at first. My sole joy was simply to make my friends, and whoever else was around, squirt milk or lager from either nostril. There were many ways to do this: I might impersonate someone nearby, the way they stood or talked; I might do an impromptu impression from the cartoons – a Jamaican Scooby-Doo, Barney Rubble swearing,

Deputy Dawg from Dudley; or I'd walk behind someone very quietly for a while and suddenly make a big noise – 'BOH!' Simplistic routes to laughter, certainly, but my friends seemed to like them.

I'd dance, sing – anything to get a reaction. I could do Elvis, Noddy Holder, Chuck Berry, Tommy Cooper, Max Bygraves, Frank Spencer, Muhammad Ali, Batman, Robin, Clement Freud, Dave Allen. Some of them sounded quite good. When my voice broke, only a few of the voices were affected, although when I sang everything had to be lowered several tones to accommodate the dropping of my meat and two veg.

I was on the highway to fame, with no GPS and absolutely no clue to where I was heading.

MY COMEDY DEBUT

The Queen Mary Ballroom was home turf for me. I had performed my impersonation of Elvis Presley there a couple of times. It was a safe place where I could stretch out and try new material.

One routine involved my dad's battered brown trilby. I used it for every impression I could think of that involved a hat – John Wayne, James Stewart, Jimmy Cagney, Humphrey Bogart. The audience at the Queen Mary were my peers; they soon became new acquaintances, people who were in on this brand-new thing: Lenny Henry, the black kid who got up on stage and did all the voices. I remember several moments when I knew things had changed. The first turning point was me and the rest of the Grazebrook Crew rocking up at The Ship and Rainbow, a pub about three miles from Dudley. It was smaller than the Queen Mary dancefloor-wise but packed to the gills on a Tuesday night and pumping with Motown, soul, funk and northern soul. A guy named Mike Hollis happened to be the DJ

79

that night, and he signalled that I should come to the stage as we walked in. I was literally scared witless. What if they didn't like me as much here as they did at the Queen Mary?

As it turned out, the audience were even more enthusiastic than my peers at the Mary. They went *nuts*! I loved it, and the taste of live performance became like a virus for me. I couldn't wait to get up on stage.

Mac, Greg and Tom supported me throughout, thrilled that we were now gaining free access to clubs that previously were costing us major coin to get in. It was brilliant. Some nights were tough, though. There were places where the crowd just didn't get it, but the lads made sure I had a drink once I decamped from the stage and they cheered me up immediately: 'Yow'm alright, chap – they never had any taste this lot . . .'

I couldn't believe how confident I was getting. Taking to the stage was never a problem. Somehow it didn't matter what I was doing, and if I improvised something, they seemed to like it even more. This was something I learnt early on – the audience loved it when you did material about actually being there with them. Of course, they liked the stuff you'd prepared, but they really reacted when you spoke about them, where they lived, the shape of the room, the bar staff, the state of the toilets. They loved the cut and thrust and banter of live performance just as much as I did. I got up and strutted my stuff, with no trace of fear or nervousness. The moment I always loved was the 'whoosh' of recognition at the voices – and also the certain knowledge that they had never seen a black person doing impersonations of people they knew from TV.

Although Mike Hollis was my main conduit to performing on stage, there were other DJs with whom I became friendly. Cliff Curry, The General and Johnny Olsen all let me get up and perform, but Mike was my main man, and I tried as hard as I could to be wherever he was playing since that meant stage time.

In many ways this period was the best of times. The constant push of getting up and trying out new material – the improvisations at the Queen Mary, watching a woman almost choke with laughter at The Fox and Goose in Kingswinford . . . I didn't realise it at the time, but these were halcyon days.

Unbeknownst to me, what I was doing was 'woodshedding' or 'workshopping' material. Fifteen-year-old Len was doing what the big-boy comedians did: before an important performance any comic worth their salt is either out on tour or doing work-in-progress shows to get the material up to scratch. I was working my material until it squeaked.

Greg, Mac, Tom and another brother, Knocker, used to have my back at all the clubs. It was fun, and we got free drinks from the owners, DJs and other interested parties. They made me feel special, even though I was still wearing hand-me-down clothes from the Army and Navy Store. For the first time, girls did not dismiss my patched-up appearance. Now they were interested. We were all in heaven. Me especially.

MIKE HOLLIS

Mike Hollis was known in the clubs by his DJ name, Oscar Michael. He was tall, handsome and always smartly turned out. The way he dressed was effortless. He didn't look like he was trying to be hip, cool and trendy – he actually was those things.

Mike was the one who spotted me. He was a resident DJ at the Queen Mary, and after I'd performed there one Sunday night he came up to me and said, 'Yow should be on the telly.' I liked Mike, the music he played and how he held the stage. I think that's why I trusted his taste and believed him.

In my autobiographical BBC film, *Danny and the Human Zoo* (2015, dir. Destiny Ekaragha), I portrayed Mike's character (called the Magnificent Jonesy in the film) as a bit of an

opportunist ne'er-do-well. But in truth, without his interven-
tion it might have taken me many, many years to get to a point
where anyone was interested in what I was doing. Mike really
was the catalyst to my career; he lit the blue touchpaper and
watched me take off.

Check out Jonesy's scenes in the film, just to see how they
capture the spirit of the Queen Mary Ballroom in those days:
the Bowie dancers, the Rod Stewart imitators, the funkateers,
the mods, the skins, the acrobats. All were consumers of the
great music that Mike played. The Queen Mary was the place
where you could express yourself, and Mike was our ringmaster.

But it wasn't just that, because even the best DJs in the world
with the best records to hand can have a duff set. Mike had
great taste and he could read a room. When things were too hot,
he'd cool us down with 'There's No Stopping Us Now' by the
Supremes. When they were too cool, he'd switch to 'Move on
Up' by Curtis Mayfield, and the floor would become packed
with movers, groovers and party people. If Mike wanted some
kind of show-stopping moment, he'd play 'There Was a Time'
by James Brown and beckon to the O'Meally brothers, who
would take command of the dancefloor, their shirts off and
sweat gleaming. The three of them would leap and cavort, roll
and rock and flik-flak across the dancefloor.

And when all else failed, Mike would tell jokes – lots of them.
He would casually fade a record out, until it was playing quietly, and say something like:

'Last night I slept like a log. I woke up in the fireplace.'

Or:

'I got stopped by a copper last night. He looked in my car and
he said, "Why've you got a bucket of water on the passenger's
seat?" I says, "So I can dip me headlights."'

These are very trad jokes. We would have heard them on the
TV or radio, on programmes like *The Tommy Cooper Show*

or from Frank Carson on *The Comedians*. But us fifteen- and sixteen-year-old kids, out for the night, drinking underage – we lapped it all up. It was as though Mike understood that this was the only night out we were liable to get this week, so we deserved everything he could throw at us.

There were other crazy-ass DJs around in those days. Barmy Barry (red-headed, moustachioed, jovial) had a record shop in Dudley and also deejayed when he felt like it. He gave away records and cracked gags, but although he was pretty good, he'd been at the game a long time and was due a rest. The General was brilliant: very glam-rock styled, David Bowie/Ziggy trim, red-haired, flowing white clothes, he hopped and skipped while addressing the kids and ran games and competitions. He really put himself out there when he was doing a show, but it wasn't about the music, it was about him.

Cliff Curry used to have the dopest sound system in the Midlands. He and Mike were good friends and they would sometimes work together at the Queen Mary. Cliff was a tall, hefty guy with blond hair and a moustache. Cliff wasn't as larky a DJ as Mike Hollis – he mostly preferred to stick to the music – but when I would get up and do my bits on his watch, he would often become infected by the sense of fun and craziness and join in. We would do a strange and chaotic ventriloquism skit, all improvised, with Cliff as the vent and me as the dummy. I have no idea what we were doing, but we made an audience of my peers and some older types roar with laughter.

After Mike saw me perform a few times, he wanted to be my manager. And because I was desperate for some/any attention from anyone, I said yes. I saw he could run things well. The way he manipulated the crowd every week through music and jokes was a sight to behold. I wanted to be part of the Oscar Michael show and followed him everywhere like a big Jamaican puppy. I figured that that way, everyone would be able to see my talent.

Mike wrote out a contract on some foolscap paper in felt-tip pen and knocked on our door at Douglas Road, wanting to meet my mama and papa. He charmed Mama into co-signing a contract with me. Contained in this contract was a section that stated he would get 33.3 per cent of all my earnings. I was so desperate to be in show business that I didn't question this. There was no Henry lawyer kindly looking over the paperwork in case there were any anomalies; just my family standing around wondering why this smoothly dressed white dude was in our house.

This contract did eventually change once it was shown to a solicitor. Mike would manage my career for ten years, but in the beginning who was I to question his business experience? He was the incredible Oscar Michael, purveyor of funky good times. He could have written that contract in spit on a burning log and I wouldn't have questioned it. I had already leapt off the cliff here – no coercion necessary.

At that time Mike was my Gandalf. He helped me buy clothes, bolstered my confidence, drove me to shows. He invited me to his home, where I met his mum, dad and grandfather, who kept pigeons. Mike's parents had a phone, an electric organ and tons of antiques lying around. I remember them being very proud of their son. I was probably the only black person who'd ever visited their house, though everyone pretended that my presence was no big deal.

Mike once told me that I was going to be bigger than Max Bygraves. I didn't really know who he was. Then I saw Bygraves at work, and I thought, 'Why him?' He seemed like someone to impersonate, not emulate. At the time, I'd been listening, at Mike's behest, to Bill Cosby's albums. They were funny, made up of two- or three-minute bits of material. Cosby would find a memory and mine it for as many laughs as he could. He didn't do jokes; instead he told stories. Initially I found this confusing

– what was it with all these stories about his childhood? And then I began to wonder, why didn't I have loads of childhood stories in my material? I loved Cosby's avuncular, sound effect-laden style, his use of the microphone, his crystallisation and embellishment of past events. I didn't know how to do that. It didn't occur to me that at sixteen years of age I was perhaps too close to my childhood to use it as material, but if I was going to aspire to be anyone, it was Cosby, although it would be at least another nine years before I could start talking about my childhood on stage or on TV. No one suspected that America's favourite dad had a dark underside; sadly, that was to emerge later.

At the time, I envied Cosby's success and secretly wanted to be like him. I'd listened to his albums and had watched him act with Robert Culp in the TV series *I Spy*. Here was a black guy holding a central role in a hit TV series. He looked like me and he was a huge, *huge* success. But Mike understood a basic truth: no obscure mimicry; I was only allowed to impersonate people that Middle England would know.

As a mentor Mike helped me with material. He collected jokes for me, continued to encourage me to listen to comedy albums and watch hit TV comedy shows. If we couldn't think of a great joke, we'd steal one, or even two, from someone else.

I wasn't a great impressionist to start with, so I knew that if the recognition factor was limited, then something else had to happen. That's the problem with impressions: once you've done (or attempted to do) the voice, then what? Dudley audiences were tough: they stood there watching, thinking, 'You better come with the laughs now, kid.'

Mike made me work on new voices. I was listening to tapes, watching television and rehearsing *in situ*. This pre-*New Faces* period of woodshedding was vital. However, a small voice inside me was saying, 'Hang on, this is something I used to do to make me mates laugh. This is like *work* or summat.' But I didn't resent the work ethic; I embraced it. If I was going to make any impact, I had to practise until the entire performance was effortless.

THE *NEW FACES* AUDITION

In the mid-1970s the UK had two TV talent shows running simultaneously: Thames Television's warhorse *Opportunity Knocks* and ATV's relatively recent ratings-winner *New Faces*. After my first couple of appearances at the Queen Mary Ballroom, Mike Hollis had written to both of them. They were popular, nationally broadcast talent shows that could easily transform a performer's career after just one or two appearances. Mike had jumped the gun; he hadn't asked me whether I wanted to go on these shows or not, but he was ahead of the curve. For a working-class black kid from Dudley show business was a locked door. I'd just been offered two keys.

Opportunity Knocks was a successful, old-school talent show that began on the BBC Light Programme in 1948 and eventually migrated to television in 1956. My family were regular viewers. The show was hosted by all-round entertainer Hughie Green, who was all puns, raised eyebrows and one-liners. He had a natural bonhomie that perhaps masked an ego the size of Brazil. But the audience loved the randomness of the applicants, who, sponsored by friends or family, grabbed their moment in the spotlight as if their lives depended on it. Did they have what it took to make it to the big time or not? There were singing dogs, comedians, a muscleman with dancing pecs, ventriloquists, pop groups and much, much more. A light entertainment pudding of a show.

The voting in the studio was monitored by something called the clap-o-meter, a cardboard circle with a needle which (supposedly) registered the volume of the audience's applause, moving from zero to one hundred, depending on the level of approval. Paul Daniels, the famed magician, commented that the needle was operated by Hughie Green's foot. However, the real voting happened via post, with the viewers writing in to say who they thought deserved to win. The Liverpudlian comic Tom O'Connor won for something like six weeks on the trot. By the time he'd finished his run, he was a national star and had secured his own variety show and a game show. Some great people were discovered on that programme: Freddie Starr, Paul Daniels, Mary Hopkin, Bobby Crush (who could reduce a grand piano to matchwood in seconds), Little and Large, Lena Zavaroni, Frank Carson, Max Boyce and Debra Stephenson, to name but a few.

New Faces began when I was about fifteen. The show was markedly different to *Opportunity Knocks* in format. A precursor of many of the shows we now see on television, the show had a panel of four well-known experts (people like music producers Tony Hatch and Mickie Most, comics Arthur Askey and Ted Ray, DJs Noel Edmonds and Terry Wogan) who sat in judgement as the aspiring superstars strutted their stuff. Marks were given for 'Presentation', 'Entertainment Value', 'Star Quality' and 'Content'. The only person to get the full 120 marks was a charismatic performer called Patti Boulaye. The talented impressionist Les Dennis got 119.

Each episode began with an animation telling the story of a street busker making it big in show business. The theme tune was catchy and tuneful, sung by Carl Wayne, formerly of the Move. The way he sang it made you want to audition immediately. I was a fan of the show before I was asked to appear. They'd already discovered people like Victoria Wood, and she was quality, so I was ready to go. I began to generate three-minute bits that were clean, that I could use to audition for *New Faces*, that were suitable for pre-watershed television.

The three-minute module was a lucky charm for me in those early days. I'd found a formula that worked and stuck to it. Afterwards, it became a bit of a noose; most top-line performers did longer than three minutes.

But Mike had other ideas. He suggested a Frank Spencer gag about suntan lotion, something I would never have done normally: 'I put on some Ambre Solaire and I can't get it off now.' I practised the line over and over. It got a huge laugh, but I didn't know why. Stupid naivety. This type of joke was the kind of thing that Charlie Williams did. Anything to do with race or colour that was self-deprecating was a way of reeling in the mainstream audience. I wasn't one of the trouble-makers; I was a friend. So I carried on listening to Mike Yarwood and collecting jokes off other comedians. I was as raw as raw could be. I had no idea that I was unique, a fifteen-year-old child of Jamaican heritage who could impersonate white people off the telly.

Luckily for me, someone from *New Faces* wrote to Mike and told him that they would be very interested to see this young black impressionist from Dudley. They gave him a date and time for an audition, and that was that. I was in. I couldn't tell my mother, though, because that would have placed a massive obstacle in my way. She would have forbidden me to go due to the fact that the auditions took place on a Friday during school hours.

I kept honing the material in the clubs, and by the time of the audition I was more than ready. I knew what I had to do, how to time it and how to finish. Mike had an idea about how I should look on stage and took me shopping in Austin Reed in Dudley: green checked jacket, patterned shirt, baggy-ish trousers with a high waistband, loafers.

I don't really have a memory of being nervous on audition day. Mike picked me up, we drove to Birmingham in his Jensen Interceptor, and some thirty minutes later we pulled up outside a scruffy club in a side street. Obviously, in the evening, with the

neon lights and the velvet rope and the smartly dressed bouncers, this place was the number-one local spot for cabaret, music,
dancing, a chicken-in-the-basket supper and then a snog in the
minicab on the way home. But like most clubs, in the daytime it
left a lot to be desired. As we made our way through the foyer,
over the sticky carpet, you could smell the stale BO, cigarettes
and, as we approached the main auditorium, the urine-soaked
gents' toilets.

It was perfect for auditions, though. There was an expanse
of stage, with plenty of room off to the sides for the numer-
ous acts to warm up and prepare. There was a large auditorium
capable of holding up to 800 audience members. The kitchen
prepared various meals in a basket for the auditionees. And here
I was, with Mike, ready to show these associate producers what
I could do.

The panel of judges sat at the front, near the stage. All they
would say was, 'NEXT!' Brutal.

This was where I became transfixed and enthralled by the
world of show business. This was a place of girl and boy singers,
comedy double acts, guitar vocalists, a cappella groups, show
bands, contortionists, fire-eaters, comedians, singing dogs,
gymnasts and drag acts. I loved it. This was where I wanted to
be for the rest of my life – or so I thought.

The day was nerve-wracking. The judges were being very particular about what they wanted in the show. There had already
been a black comic who started telling a joke, and before he
even reached the punchline . . . 'NEXT!' There was a comedy
show band. The lead singer was an impressionist very much in
the Russ Abbot style, and I thought he was funny (particularly
his Columbo), but . . . 'NEXT!'

This went on all day, but I didn't care. I was learning so much
about performance, confidence, poise and stature. These performers really knew how to take it to the stage; somehow it

didn't matter what the judges thought. I loved the way everyone had practised what they were going to do to the point of boredom. It worked against them sometimes. Some acts perform as though their show is the least interesting thing about them. I have never been sure about this approach: if you're not interested, why should we be? Yet Steve Martin made a living from being so laid back he was practically horizontal.

Finally, it's 6 p.m., and at last my name gets called. I realise that I don't have a Tommy Cooper hat, the iconic fez. Luckily, there are so many impressionists that not only am I able to borrow a proper fez, but I also have a choice of colour, from plum to scarlet to orange. I go for the scarlet one.

I get up on stage, and I'm nervous because I'll be performing to a packed audience of performers, either waiting to do their bit or having already performed. Luckily, I had no idea how tough a pro crowd could be. I begin the audition and, at first, I'm speeding through the material – but then, time stops. I am able to just . . . pause in my mind before each bit, each impression. It's the most in control I've ever been. I wonder where that has come from? The confidence, the zest and vigour? It's almost as if I've been possessed by someone or something else. The drive to succeed. I feel strangely unassailable up there, like it is meant to be. What a glorious feeling.

I pour everything into the first three minutes. There are laughs and rounds of applause. I continue – no one says, 'NEXT!' Six minutes, seven, eight . . . I'm running out of material and the laughs keep coming and no one is saying, 'NEXT!' In the end I just bow, and the audience stand up, clap their hands and cheer.

Absolutely, no shadow of a doubt, this is one of the most brilliant moments of my life. But even faced with a standing ovation and a cheering crowd, I am so scared and worried about whether I've done well or not that in my mind the whole thing has just slid by in an instant. As I descend the stairs away from the stage, a group of theatrical agents, wannabe managers and rapscallions run down to congratulate me:

'That was great, kid.'

'How old am ya again?'

'Take my card and give me a ring.'

'I think I know how to turn you into a star.'

I look out for Mike, who is barging his way through all these johnny-come-latelys and taking control of the situation. He accepts the proffered cards and yells, 'If any pillock here wants to book *my* client, Lenny Henry, they'll have to go through me!'

Then, as if by magic, we are back in the car with big stupid smiles on our faces, on our way home to Dudley.

Audition done and dusted.

Who Am I #4

I love this picture. I'm mid-act on New Faces. *I'm wearing clothes from Bird Cage Walk in Dudley, all chosen by Mike Hollis. The bow tie doesn't quite work with the shirt, but it doesn't seem to matter. You can tell by my eyes that I'm completely involved in, and focused on, what I'm supposed to be doing. I'm doing Windsor Davies from* It Ain't Half Hot Mum *here. Now, all I can think is, 'Christ, I was such a kid! What did I think I was doing?' (Shutterstock)*

BUT BACK HOME . . .

Mike dropped me off outside my house and zoomed off. He had seen my mother's silhouette in the front window and didn't want to deal with her. I got to the door, full of confidence and joy, all of which leaked away as soon as I saw her face. This was a 'Len about to get knocked through a brick wall' moment.

Mama opens the front door. Looks at her watch. Glares at me. Says, 'Where you bin?'

Me: 'Audition.'

Mama: '*Which* audition?'

Me: 'For *New Faces* – in Birmingham.'

Mama: 'On a school day? You mad? In your Sunday School clothes!'

Me: 'I got through. I'm gonna be on telly!'

A pause as she takes it all in.

Mama: 'Humph. What you do down there?'

Me: 'Impressions.'

Mama: 'Do it for me now.'

Me: 'What?'

Mama: 'If you wan' come in the house and eat your dinner tonight, you do this audition for me right now!'

So I did:

(as Tommy Cooper, red fez on head) '*I went to the doctor the other day. He said, "Take off all your clothes and stand by the window." I said, "Why?" He said, "I can't stand my neighbours."*'

(with floppy hands and dour face – Max Bygraves) '*Here's a funny story. I went to the dentist. He said, "Say ahhhh." I said, "Why?" He said, "My dog died this morning."*'

(with Groucho Marx moustache, eyebrows and glasses) '*I was married by a judge. I should have asked for a jury!*'

(as Frank Spencer, wearing the beret) *'I had a ploughman's lunch the other day. He was furious.'*

Mama and my brothers and sisters behind her were all applauding! This was almost better than the audition. My family had reacted positively to something they hadn't seen before – me doing impressions. It was sweet.

I was genuinely surprised by their reaction. This was something that previously I'd done only for people who knew me: Greg, Mac, Tom and the rest of the lads; the people down the park; the punters in the Queen Mary Ballroom and at the Trapper's Bar. But never for my family. The secret was out now. I wasn't just some lanky, goofy kid from the Buffery; suddenly, they saw that I might just possibly have a career in show business.

Who Am I #5

Brian Moody, an excellent photographer, came up to Dudley
in 1974 to get pictures of this kid who'd just auditioned and
won a place on New Faces. My favourite shot is this one of
myself, Mama, my Auntie Pearl and the kids – Paul, Sharon (in
a very nice Sunday School dress), Auntie Pearl's son, Adrian,
and Kay's son, Justin. I'm in big Oxford bags, tank top and
round-collared shirt. Mama and Auntie Pearl are wearing
Blaxploitation-style Afro wigs. Mama looks happy. So does
Auntie Pearl. Though I look happy, I think I'm realising that
the appearance on New Faces has implications not just for
myself, but for my family too.

    With Danny and the Human Zoo, I understood that
elements of my life would be appropriated for the film (it is a

WHO AM I, AGAIN?

*fictionalised representation of the first two years of my career),
which is fine if you have no family. But when you're writing
about yourself at age fifteen, you have to remember that
you're also writing about your family members. After* Danny
and the Human Zoo *was aired, all of my siblings were hassled
by the press on their doorsteps, walking from the shops and
even by letters slid under the door. This picture reminds me
of a time when I was slowly realising what fame could mean:
not just an invasion of my privacy, but of everybody else's too.
(Brian Moody)*

THE APPRENTICESHIP

I knew things had changed after the audition. When people found out about it, they insisted that I get up and perform. Even our English teacher and form master, Ron 'Bomber' Nash, who had previously ignored me for most of my school career, told me during a careers consultation that since I was going to be in show business, I didn't have to worry about my future – which I thought was irresponsible. What if it didn't work out? What if I got kicked out of show business before I'd even begun? It would be his fault if forty years later I was staggering around Dudley High Street in my pyjamas, rummaging through the bins round the back of Greggs.

I was asked to perform in the school concert. I didn't even know they had one. Suddenly, at the age of fifteen, I was allowed to do two fifteen-minute sets and compère the whole thing. I was over the moon – my journey had been legitimised by Blue Coat secondary modern! The *Express and Star* even came to the school and took pictures of me entertaining my classmates. The concert went pretty well, considering I'd never compèred before. I remember having a great time and soaking up the laughter and applause as if they were oxygen. Why hadn't I done this before? Performing was life-affirming, a clear sign from the gods that there was a future for me that did not involve learning about welding or metalwork or carpentry and such. I was *almost* free. But not quite: there was a time lag between the auditions and the actual recording of my appearance on *New Faces*. They made me wait till I was sixteen.

I left school with seven CSEs, which was the equivalent of a fireguard made of Cadbury's Dairy Milk. So, while waiting to reach the age when I could appear on television, I took the entrance exam for Dudley Technical College and, surprisingly, did really well. However, I chose instead to go to West Bromwich Technical College, because that was where most of my school chums were going. Also, by attending classes there I was entitled to an apprenticeship at British Federal Welders, which was an enormous factory complex about five minutes from Dudley Zoo. It sat on about three acres and was smokey, dark and testosterone-laden, with blokes in overalls *everywhere*. Female employees seemed to work only in the offices or canteen.

I received a six-week induction at the factory. I made friends with Derek, who became my mentor throughout the apprenticeship process. In the space of six weeks he tutored me on assembling a spot-welding machine from scratch. He was patient, kind and an excellent teacher. I'm pretty sure I was a hopeless student with no attention span, but by the end of the six weeks I could just about put one of those machines together.

I wore ill-fitting overalls, and like almost everyone that worked there I bunked off at various times during the day, hiding in the toilet, reading the *Daily Mirror* and daydreaming about being famous. I saw myself arriving at posh nightclubs, a gorgeous model on my arm, drinking champagne and eating teeny-tiny food on sticks. I liked the ridiculously big food my mother made, but I was willing to try anything. This reverie was usually interrupted by Derek banging on the bog door: 'Oi, y'lazy bastard! Get your arse out of there and back to work!'

Factory work was gruelling and unending. I don't know how my papa got through it every day. He worked at Bean's Industries for over thirty years, and when he came home he rarely smiled or spoke about what had happened that day. I didn't want to be trapped like that, and I certainly didn't intend to stay at 'the Federal'. But once there, we all seemed to be welded to a one-way track, our journeys apparently marked out for us. Induction, college, qualifications, and then back to the Federal for the rest of our working lives; wife, kids, mortgage, overdraft, eventual death . . . So I made extra sure to keep practising my impressions. Once I'd taken the leap into the world of light entertainment, I really didn't want to go back to factory life. But I still hadn't heard anything from the *New Faces* production team and was convinced that they had forgotten about me.

There were distractions at college. We were near West Bromwich Albion's football ground and sometimes we'd sneak into the pub nearby and see some of the players relaxing after training; to be so close to these local soccer legends was amazing. There were new people to meet and appraise. The only girl on our course was called Heather. She had a perm, and even though she was our age, she seemed older and wiser than us. She was a brilliant engineer in the making; her technical-drawing skills were superb. I was in awe of her – probably the first relationship with a member of the opposite sex where I wasn't thinking about snogging. Heather would look over my drawings and point out where my draughtsmanship had gone awry. I was extremely grateful for her help. Everyone else seemed to have it covered – and even if they didn't, they wouldn't tell you. They were guys, after all.

I performed the same function at college as I did over in the park or at school: whenever there was an opportunity, I would mess around, do voices, tell jokes. It was different here, though, because these guys hadn't experienced what I'd been doing. I just threw them into the deep end. Dave and Johnny weren't that impressed; they thought that I was just a show-off and probably hadn't auditioned for *New Faces*. Cecil and Wesley were cool and had my back throughout my time at West Brom Tech.

Racism would rear its head occasionally. At college my principal tormentor was Barry Jones, who took it upon himself to remind everyone that I was a coon/nig-nog/darkie scum who stank, etc. He'd mutter it under his breath or talk about me behind my back till I walked in the room, and then he'd stop. He'd even say things to my face on occasion. Being on the receiving end of this kind of sustained ignorance is tiresome. As usual, I tried joking my way out of it by playing to the gallery. Sometimes it worked:

(as David Bellamy, enthusiastically mispronouncing my 'r's) '*Here I am at West Bwomich, just outside Bwum, and I'm cwouched down, appwoximately thwee feet from the lesser spotted Jones. Now pweviously we have noticed that this cweature is, in mywiad ways, twoubled and uneducated, but we've wecently come to the conclusion that he's just a wacist pwick.*'

Barry would shout at me, the guys would laugh, and then there'd be a squabble followed by a nearly-fight: all the guys and Heather would gather round, and Barry and I would square up to each other and yell in each other's faces. Nothing ever came of it; it was just the way things were in the mid-1970s.

And then one day he called me a 'black c*nt'.

We were in a class, wearing our overalls, toiling over the lathes. It was boring, and I was imitating Barry's every word for the amusement of the group. Eventually, Barry lost his rag, turned on me and spat out the offending phrase. My cheeks burnt. I was really upset – I'd been called this offensive name before, but only up the football by the opposing fans, who didn't like it that West Brom had the Three Degrees: Laurie Cunningham, Cyrille Regis and Brendon Batson, three black players who performed feats of magic on the pitch despite all the racist abuse people would throw at them. I admired that.

But I wasn't them. I lashed out and caught Barry with a whopping blow to the side of his face. And unlike the heroes of the action films that I'd devoured as a kid, I didn't pile in with a second punch because my fist was now aching like crazy. It pulsed and throbbed like I was in a Warner Bros cartoon. I could feel it swelling up, and the pain was enormous. Meanwhile, Barry had left the room, holding his face. Everyone gathered round and told me that he'd had it coming, he was a racist twat, he deserved it. But I just felt sad that I'd lashed out; there had to be a better way of settling differences. What happened to what I'd learnt at school about handling racism with humour?

I don't remember precisely what happened after that. I wasn't reported to the lecturers or excluded. Life just went on, with Barry and I giving each other a wide berth, and things settled down.

THE FIRST WORKING MEN'S CLUBS

In the meantime, I was trying out new material in the evenings, with Greg, Mac and, sometimes, Tom in attendance. The guys would take me to the discos, but also to places like Bilston Steel Working Men's Club – just to get a taste of what a grown-up entertainment venue was like. The club was overlooked by a massive, smoke-belching steelworks; the soot and grime from the chimneys settled everywhere, and all the cars in the car park were coated with a patina of black dust.

When we entered the venue, we were the youngest people by a country mile. It was grim: post-war décor, patterned wall-paper, sticky brown carpet, beer-stained wooden bar, with wooden taps for the beer and ancient bags of pork scratchings, crisps and nuts pinned to the wall. The bar staff were all old and white; everyone chain-smoked. A constant stream of show tunes pootled out from the speakers as some ancient keyboardist played on a tiny stage, far away in the corner. He was to be my accompanist. I'd spent some money on an Elvis Presley song-book that had the chords for all his songs. I thought it might be a worthwhile investment. Turned out I was wrong. Most of the accompanists in the working men's clubs could read a bit of music, but not particularly well. They could play the chords, but they never played what you wanted. They played what they could, and you just had to hang in there.

So I handed the keyboard player my music. I was going to do some impressions, but I would also sing 'Blue Suede Shoes' and 'Jailhouse Rock' to 'top and tail' the set. There was some confusion: I'd been listening to these records my entire life, but what the man was playing did not resemble them in any way, shape or form. At many band rehearsals over the next few years I would find myself trying to explain how a record went, and the musician would nod and then play his version of what I'd just said, which would bear no resemblance to any music I'd ever heard before or since, leaving me to improvise around whatever they played.

Bilston Steel was the first place where I felt a seed of doubt pushing its way firmly into my gut. The audience, all white, all middle-aged and older, didn't appreciate what I was doing in the same way the younger audiences at the discos had. They laughed at Frank Spencer and Tommy Cooper, but they didn't laugh at Muhammad Ali. It was the first time I'd been disappointed by my performance. It hadn't been fun.

So I went back and had another go, but this time on my own. I figured I'd better get used to going to these types of places, because this was the real world.

I was living a dual existence. By day I attended West Bromwich Technical College and served my apprenticeship at British Federal Welders, and by night I performed in every discotheque that would allow me up on stage: Club Montesa, The Saracen's Head, The Ship and Rainbow, The Fox and Goose, the Queen Mary Ballroom, Club Lafayette – anywhere with a stage and a curious DJ.

THE CALL

And then, just before Christmas 1974, I got the news. I'm not sure exactly how it was conveyed to me. It could have been a phone call, but then I don't remember us having a phone (I might have bought our first phone several years later). It could have been sky-written by a light aircraft overhead, but I'm not sure who would have paid for that. Certainly not Mike Hollis, and definitely not ATV. Let's say, for argument's sake, that Mike gave me the news at the Queen Mary Ballroom: I was going to be on television in January 1975. The *New Faces* production team had called him, telling him that I had to get a decent three minutes together, wear proper showbiz-type clothes, with no swearing, and please be punctual. Light blue touchpaper and stand back.

The show was to be pre-recorded on the Tuesday, so Mike and I went down to ATV's studios in Birmingham on the Monday just to orient ourselves with the production team.

When you go to a working TV studio, things happen all around you. That Monday, when we walked in for the stagger-through, I saw members of the *Crossroads* cast and was thrilled but also shocked at how people look behind the scenes. There's Amy Turtle in rollers. There's Sandy Richardson out of his wheelchair. There's Meg Richardson – she's like a flame-haired goddess in slingbacks. I got to run my hands over the reception desk of the Crossroads motel, until the security guy told me to 'move along, lad, none of this is here for your entertainment'.

I also got to walk on the set of *The Golden Shot*, where I met the show's host, Bob Monkhouse, a brilliant comedian with the memory of an elephant. Monkhouse was a student of comedy who taped every comedy radio show and videoed the debut set of every comic working on television. He knew everyone's act. When I met him again years later, he still knew every joke I'd used in my debut performance and recited them back to me. When I appeared on *The Golden Shot*, he stood by my side and helped me to improvise the whole thing on the spot.

For some reason, ATV did not keep the tapes of the original series of *New Faces*, so all the debut performances of Jim Davidson, Victoria Wood, Showaddywaddy, Sweet Sensation, the Chuckle Brothers, Marti Caine, etc., had, to all intents and purposes, been lost. I'd been searching for my first appearance on the show for some time, but no one could locate a video, VHS or Beta. And then in 2016 one of the producers of *New Faces*, Paul Stewart Laing, called me and asked if I wanted to see my debut on the programme. I thought he might be teasing me. I told Paul that no one had a copy of that show, and he said, 'Bob Monkhouse had a pristine video in his cellar.' Monkhouse had taped the 1975 series of *New Faces* in its entirety and had kept the videos in a massive archive in his cellar. Paul invited me to a screening of that first show, and I was incredibly moved. My memory – fractured and blurred at best – snapped into focus the minute I sat next to Paul and they rolled the tape.

THE REVEAL

I'd chosen my show clothes with Mike's help. Once again I'd gone to Austin Reed on Birdcage Walk in Dudley and had selected a beige checked jacket, a Viking-encrusted shirt with a big round collar, and some Oxford bags. My props – Frank Spencer hat and mac, etc. – had all been picked out and were ready to go. I'd worked and worked and worked on my routine until it was gleaming and I could do it in my sleep.

The producers were great and offered lighting- and camera-based advice: 'Maybe deliver this line here . . . This is your edge of frame . . . You don't have to yell that particular bit because you're right under the boom mic,' etc. All handy stuff to know.

I can't remember exactly who was on *New Faces* that day, but I do recall there was a ventriloquist, a Tom Jones-style singer, a black female vocalist and a band of some sort. It was very exciting watching how they put the programme together. I'd assumed that television was something that just happened: the performers made up their lines on the spot. This was the day I found out that *everything* had a structure. Links had been written, a camera script had been produced, there was a beginning, middle and end to everything.

John Pullen, an executive on the programme, came and spoke to me after my first rehearsal:

'Well done, lad. Very funny!'

'Thank you.'

'It's John. I'm one of the producers.'

I pulled a face that said, 'I don't know what that means.'

'I'm here to help. Look, instead of facing the cameras and the audience when you start doing Frank Spencer, why don't you start with your back to the audience? That way you'll have a reveal when you turn around.'

I had no idea what a 'reveal' was, but I did as I was told. Mike thought it was a good idea. So, on the night, I changed my opening. I'd start with my back to the cameras and then turn around . . .

Derek Hobson, a Northern Irish presenter, was the lynchpin of the show. He introduced me as 'a Dudley lad aged sixteen . . .' And then I was on, back to the audience, doing my Frank Spencer impression. The audience laughed a bit, not too much, though. I hadn't done any gags yet . . . just babbling about the baby . . . And then I turned round to face the cameras and the audience.

And that's when my life changed forever.

The impact of starting with my back to the cameras became clear as I turned to face everyone – and the audience discovered I wasn't just another impressionist. I was a young Afro-Caribbean, British-born lad from Dudley. I was black.

And they hadn't known.

Mama's h'integration thing had been drummed into me so well I'd almost forgotten it. But now, as I ran through my material, I was hyper-aware that something else was going on here. The material was fine. A lot of it was jokes we'd all heard before; some of it was me attempting to craft a narrative, a riff on cartoons, a riff on *Some Mothers Do 'Ave 'Em*. There were applause breaks, big laughs, and finally a huge round of applause at the end. The audience had really enjoyed it.

Watching the performance all those years later, I saw in my youthful eyes the commitment to this new life. It took huge chutzpah to stand there, aged sixteen, and go, 'Here I am, have this.' I sat there in tears, watching that kid and thinking, 'Where did that come from?'

And then it was all over. Three minutes whizz by in performance. However, internally it's slow slow slow as you pick and choose pace, inflection, meaning. During the set, everything should be calm. There shouldn't be any panic, no rushing, because you've worked the material to such an extent that it's just there at your fingertips.

I think my reaction to the judges' marks and comments was genuine. We're so used to seeing the judges on *X Factor* and *The Voice* chatting away with the contestants that we forget that back in the day it was different. On *New Faces* the judges ruled, and they spoke about you as if you weren't present. Tony Hatch and Mickie Most were renowned for their blunt appraisals. They made grown men and women cry with their comments. My appraisal on *New Faces*, luckily, was very positive. I got good marks and lovely comments from all the judges – and then suddenly I'd won.

Now everyone knew who I was. But did I?

Greg and Mac were in the audience that night. They congratulated me, and we went to Club Lafayette in Wolverhampton to celebrate. It was a brilliant night. I drank and danced and couldn't stop. I was adrenalised. If this was showbiz, bring it on. I wanted more! I didn't want this to end. I closed my eyes and jumped.

Who Am I #6

The white heat of New Faces. *It's the very first thing: me doing Michael Crawford's Frank Spencer. Every time I see this picture, I'm reminded of that day at the ATV studios: my family and friends in the audience, sausage, egg and chips in the canteen, being backstage with all the other contestants. And then the host, Derek Hobson, announces my name, the lights come on, and I hit the stage. Three minutes of white noise. I was like one of those mums who, after a terrible car accident,*

the rear axle snapped in two, lifts the car single-handedly, rescues the kids, drags the car to a safe place and somehow manages to get to a public phone box to call the AA. And then afterwards, when they're asked about what happened, they can't remember. When I look at this photograph – and indeed when I rewatched my first three minutes on television – I see a kid wearing a mask of complete and utter focus. I don't think I've concentrated so hard in my entire life. This was a sink or swim moment. I knew that, so I wasn't fooling around. I was sixteen – where did that determination come from? It certainly didn't hang around. There were many times afterwards when my focus wavered and my confidence snuck out of the back door, moments when I choked. But that didn't happen here. (Shutterstock)

The day after, I went back to West Brom Tech and didn't tell anyone that I'd won. I thought I'd savour the feeling of being just another student, apprenticed to the British Federal Welders' factory for just a few more days. The guys who knew I'd gone to Birmingham to make my TV debut were convinced I'd lost or embarrassed myself. I managed to conceal my delight for a whole week. And then transmission day came around.

The whole family sat in front of the TV and watched the show. They all went nuts. As the performance unfolded, they kept looking at the TV and then back at me, as if the whole thing had been planned as an elaborate hoax. Mama was entranced by the show, incredibly moved and moist-eyed throughout. My papa didn't say much, although he did pat me on the shoulder afterwards, grunting, 'Mek sure yu keep yu feet on the ground,' as he passed by on his way into the kitchen.

Everyone was really happy for me, and then at the end of the show, once I'd been pronounced the winner, I did some weird stuff with my eyes and waved and mouthed, 'Hello, Mama.' That was it for me, I was destined for the big portion of meat for life: I had acknowledged Mama on TV in front of 16 million viewers. All that heartache, all that 'h'integration', the back-breaking hard work that she'd put into travelling to this country, setting up a home for the family, often doing several jobs to get enough money to feed us all – all of this had come to fruition.

From that moment on, her attitude towards me changed, and it took some getting used to. People would say to her in the street, 'I saw your Lenny on telly on Sat'day,' and Mama would have to think who Lenny was, because Lenny was my 'outside the house' identity. I was like Clark Kent: at home I was Len (Kal-El), one of the many Jamaican people occupying that space; outside the house I was Lenny (Superman), behaving and speaking in a completely different way to how I did at home.

Lenny was my public face, and now it'd been confirmed: this was going to be my life from now on. And I had no idea how difficult it would be.

5
Entering Showbiz

THE SUMMER SHOW

I was very naive in thinking that once I'd won *New Faces*, the work would just flow in, the BBC would bestow a TV series upon me, and ITV would knock on our door at teatime and just hurl money at us. I didn't realise that this was only the beginning. *New Faces* had a winners' final on which I had to perform, then there was a 'viewers' winners' performance, so I had to prepare more material, more impressions. In my second performance I impersonated Al Jolson, using thick white tape to mimic his minstrel lips. Not the best of my ideas. I came second by one point to a very funny, really thin Liverpudlian comic called Al 'I have to run around in the shower to get wet' Dean. I was so angry with myself. Luckily, the viewers voted that I should come back and perform again – and this time I won.

Then I was asked to be part of *The Summer Show*, a sketch show featuring acts from *New Faces*. It was a summer replacement show and would be made at Elstree, near London. The other members of the cast were singer Trevor Chance, comic Nicky Martyn, singer Charlie James (very tiny and seductive, slept in a matchbox), Victoria Wood (singer/songwriter/genius), Marti Caine (singer, comic, chain-smoker) and impressionist Aiden J. Harvey.

Now I was in this new world where it was taken as a matter of trust that I could 'come up with the goods' each time. But the truth of the matter is, I was adrift from the minute I stopped trying out material in discotheques. This condition would last for quite a long time. However, there was this weird feeling of

'Chap, y'can stop bustin' a gut now, yow'm in showbiz!' Now I was working with Dick Vosburgh and Bryan Blackburn, the writers on *The Summer Show*, who helped shape my material for each episode. Mike Hollis had suggested that for the *New Faces* final at the Palladium later that year, I should splash out and use Mike Yarwood's key writer, Spike Mullins. The process of teaching myself about creating material, about performance, etc., abruptly went on hold.

I said yes to everything and anything. I was having a ball. Now that I was famous, I got into all the discos for nothing and almost never had to buy a drink. I was 'that black guy off the telly who did impressions'. I performed for free to all my new-found friends and went through a period of not seeing Greg, Mac and Tom very much. I had been seduced by fame. I hadn't meant for this to occur; it had just happened while I wasn't looking, and no one was telling me my behaviour was wrong.

So I plunged headlong into *The Summer Show*. Vosburgh, Blackburn and the rest worked up material for us to do, and we all reacted in the same way. The singers were cool because they just had to sing, but the comics were in uproar – the material wasn't funny, topical or relevant. We had to work really hard to make ourselves believe that this material would work. The upside was that we all got to spend time together in a rehearsal room. It was fun. Suddenly I was working with adults who swore, drank, smoked and made inappropriate comments about everything. We had an extremely flamboyant director called Peter Harris, who tried his best, but we chattered and mis-behaved so much that eventually he threw a chair at us.

Because I was a kid, I was oblivious to whatever tensions there were during rehearsals. Leslie Crowther was the guest host on our first show. He was a juggernaut of British televi-sion, a comic, an actor, a singer, a sketch performer. He was incredibly impressive as a human being, very kind. I took to him immediately and followed him round like a puppy, asking him questions all the time. He was generous with his advice and taught me all kinds of things about timing, acting drunk and learning my lines. I realised that most of my elders were happy to be asked about the craft and would gladly take the time to tell me what I needed to know. I vowed from that day forth to be a sponge, to sit at the knees of my elders and betters and beg, borrow and steal words of wisdom about the profession. I needed to: the business was rough in the mid-1970s and my future path – the working men's clubs, the big clubs, the summer seasons and so on – would prove a rocky testing ground. I needed all the help I could get.

During *The Summer Show*, I watched various methodologies at work. Trevor Chance was a great singer, but he could also move a bit and do sketches. He and Nicky Martyn got on like a house on fire; they'd obviously worked with each other before. Aiden J. Harvey was a brilliant impressionist, but it was what he did in between the impressions that was genius. He had an almost staggery, Tommy Cooper-ish approach to his performance that I found captivating. The act was key, but it was like he was throwing it away as he performed. The running commentary between himself and the audience was kept up throughout.

Marti Caine was a big figure, in and among it all. She smoked fags and cracked gags with her husband, Malcolm, and whoever else was in earshot. She charmed everyone. Marti even got Victoria Wood to write material for her appearance in the winners' final at the Palladium. I don't think she used it, but it was a massive vote of confidence in Vic. Marti was sort of team leader: she was a grown-up and had worked in every wretched venue around the country. She knew what was what and wasn't gonna take any crap from anyone. Charlie James was the team chanteuse, diminutive, sexy. To me she was unattainable, unapproachable – out of my league.

Victoria was a quiet epiphany throughout the recording of *The Summer Show*. She was incredibly shy and barely spoke to anyone. She would talk to me because I was the youngest. She'd tell me how difficult it was to write a new song every week, how she wasn't that keen on the material. She missed being at home in her jim-jams, but she joined in with the big fun of rehearsals and costume fittings – and the naughtiness too. She and Marti were as thick as thieves, laughing together a lot. We all did.

Vic had the best deal in that she wrote a song every week, and each time her offering would take your breath away. My two favourites were a song about children's TV and another that went, 'Never spend a fortnight on a health farm, you'll end up with fourteen days of health.' She was a marvel: every week she'd be behind schedule, and yet the night before the recording she'd quickly produce a new song. She was truly talented and severely underused on *The Summer Show*. They just didn't know what to do with her.

By the time we'd reached the end of our contracts, I'd been away from Dudley for over two months, the longest I'd ever been separated from my close friends and family. This was a pattern that would remain unchanged for years and years and years. 'Show business' seemed to be another term for separation, isolation – and loneliness. The qualities needed to survive were a thick skin and the ability to form friendships and alliances quickly. I was learning fast.

My *Summer Show* family disbanded with promises that we'd all remain in touch, but we never did, although whenever I saw Victoria she spoke of that experience fondly and reminded me of odd moments from our time together.

The *New Faces* winners' show at the London Palladium came and went too. Marti Caine won, a group called Ofanchi came second, Al Dean came third and I came fourth. I shared a dressing room with a cockney piano-playing comic called Mike.

He taught me to meditate and get my mind right for the performance. Thank God he was there, because my manager, Mike Hollis, had kept well out of the way. He was absent throughout the whole *Summer Show* experience, offering no help or guidance during the entire series, and after the Palladium he sort of disappeared.

It wasn't really his fault. I think managing acts is a rare skill; you've either got it or you haven't. To be a good manager demands attention to detail, caring for the act, nurturing them, making them practise and sharpen their performance, helping to ensure the material is top quality, offering a shoulder to cry on. Through no fault of his own, Mike couldn't hope to deliver on the majority of these functions.

Who Am I #7

This is me, Nicky Martyn and Charlie James in The Summer
Show. *As you can see, we are dressed as the Flower Pot Men. The
mask I'm wearing here is kind of 'I don't know what the hell
I'm doing in this sketch.' I was literally going with the flow here.*

I had a nice time during The Summer Show, *being mentored
alternately by Nicky Martyn, Marti Caine and Aiden J. Harvey,
so there was no shortage of advice. But this was a real marking-
time period, as we all tried to figure out our next steps. Mine, of
course, would involve a face-down power dive into the world of
the Black and White Minstrels, but I didn't know this yet.*

WORKING THE CLUBS

The *New Faces* winners' final was not a huge victory for me, but I was still up there in a sky-blue suit in front of millions of TV viewers, performing at the fabled London Palladium. Once it was all over, I returned to the grindstone and stuck my nose down.

I was being booked to perform at working men's clubs on a regular basis. A lot of them paid cash and didn't care that I was inexperienced at playing to a demanding audience. They were incredibly hard work, and I was just thrown in at the deep end. I had a lot of rough nights when the act didn't go well, but sometimes the audience would be charmed and allow me to find my feet. On these occasions I would 'mess around' and talk to them – an embryonic attempt at improvisation. I sometimes had a feeling on stage that the fact that I was there was somehow more important than what I'd rehearsed.

In this early part of my career I was often desperate for something to happen: for a table to fall over or a mic not to work or a heckler – something I could react to that would allow my comedy to kick in. I tended to be funny in the moment, when stuff went wrong. However, my approach to the act – a mix of familiar jokes, impressions and Charlie Williams-type patter – was a problem. It dragged and didn't ever really take off. The audiences smelt blood.

It was now that my relationship with Mike began to unravel. I was doing shows in working men's clubs all over the Midlands and beyond, but Mike was working too, deejaying most nights of the week. It became clear to me that my career came second to his dreams and aspirations. I wasn't dumped or mistreated or anything like that; it's just that Mike didn't really come to any of the gigs. He did at the start – when I was asked to do a Sunday concert at the Blackpool Opera House in 1975, he and his trusty sidekick

David Luton attended. But when I was doing the journeyman stuff, schlepping from one side of the country to the other and expiring nightly at working men's clubs, Mike was nowhere to be seen. He was off deejaying all over the Midlands, while also making endless audition tapes for the BBC. I eventually realised that I would be ploughing a lonely furrow for some time.

Kev Jones, a local milkman and friend of Mike's, would sometimes drive me to gigs, but that didn't last very long. Kev was a nice guy, but he couldn't offer what I really needed. He didn't go through the show with me or offer jokes or come up with solutions to duff atmospheres and audiences. The amazing thing is that I stayed with Mike for nearly ten years. I think I was timid and thought:

'What happens if I leave? No one else will want me.'

'I'm no good. Winning *New Faces* was a fluke.'

'If it wasn't for Mike Hollis, I wouldn't be here.'

And so on . . .

One of the big obstacles to moving on was the simple fact that Mama had co-signed our contract. It was legally binding, and I didn't have the first idea about how to get out of it.

Later on, Pauline, Mike's wife, took over my day-to-day care. She was lovely throughout this whole experience. She was coping with a hormonal teenager who had just been thrust into the limelight, and I'm sure she had no idea what she was letting herself in for. But she made sure I got to gigs on the right days and at the right times, remembered to pick up my payments, got my clothes ironed pre-gig, ensured my music was collected from Colin Campbell's house (Colin wrote all the music for my shows back then), always booked taxis to take me to the train station wherever I was, etc. Pauline was brilliant and became close to my family. Later, during my mother's last few years of illness, she did everything she could to help me ensure Mama's care was viable.

I realise now that Mike had thought only of the beginning of my career and hadn't really considered the subsequent navigation, strategising and nurturing. As a fan of the 1974 film *Stardust*, I had expected Mike to be like the manager played by Adam Faith, who was hell-bent on doing whatever he could to keep David Essex's rock star in the public eye. Mike's apparent abandonment was hurtful because it didn't fit into the movie template of 'how to be a manager'. There was no self-sacrifice, no deals, no hustling to get the right gig at the right time. It was all very mundane and accepting, taking any old offer, doing any old gig, not paying very much attention and then leaving it to the wife when it all got too overwhelming.

I don't blame him. I was a young black comic with no experience of the wider world or of show business, no stage time to speak of and no way of generating material. These things take time to overcome, and Mike didn't have that because he was busy making his own way in the world. It's hard enough trying to break into this industry on behalf of someone, but to try and make your own bones simultaneously is nigh on impossible.

Lots of people criticised the way my affairs were run in the 1970s, but without Mike it would have taken much longer for me to get started. There was no one else in Dudley at the time who was like him, no one else who provided an intersection between music, jokes and show business. Because I'd seen him work the stage with such grace and competence, I knew that there was a place on that stage for me. So a tip of the hat to Mike.

ARE YOU TRIFLING WITH ME?

Things were happening in 1975, though. Mike and I had been summoned to London to meet Robert Luff, an entrepreneur/impresario who ran various summer seasons around the country. There were plans in the offing. We drove down to London in Mike's Jenson Interceptor. Mike sought to impress me by slamming his foot down on the accelerator continually and saying things like, 'Good innit, chap?'

We vroomed our way around London like Jackie Stewart and arrived at the Portman Hotel in plenty of time. The Portman in 1975 was regal in its appearance. The staff wore liveried uniforms, all purples and golds, with the bellboys in tiny hats. The frock-coated concierge showed us into the sumptuous main restaurant.

I don't think I'd ever seen a dining room like it. Everyone seemed to be dressed for fine dining. The men were in Savile Row suits, their hair neatly cut and Brylcreemed; the women were all dressed in couture outfits that dazzled and sizzled. We were totally overwhelmed. The maître d' conveyed us smoothly to Mr Luff's table, and there he was, pinstripe-suited and booted, his arms outstretched. He was the perfect English gentleman. He was a man of a certain era, sixty-ish at the time, and the consummate host, ordering wine and making sure we had menus and fizzy water. He spoke to me as an adult and didn't patronise me at all. He treated Mike as an equal in business, as though this was just a formality, the deal already done.

Meanwhile, I was fascinated by the carvery trolley, which was wheeled around the room silently, like a small tram laden with steaming joints of meat. My mother had already told me what I would eat – steak. 'Well done. Mek sure dem cook it good.' I wound up having a Steak Diane, which came in a thick gravy and was accompanied by potatoes and green beans. No dumplin' or green banana here; this was a gourmet-style restaurant. I did miss my mother's food when I was away from home, and this period was marked by my continued absence from Dudley. I had begun putting on weight and had gained half a stone by the end of the year, causing me to join a gym and embark on a ridiculous diet, eating lettuce for weeks on end until I lost a little timber. This gradual see-sawing in my bodyweight would continue for the next thirty years.

But at this particular moment I'm nearly seventeen and loving being at a classy hotel eating fancy chow. I'm not really paying attention to what the grown-ups are saying; I'm looking at the posh décor. One roll of wallpaper here cost more than our entire house. I had eaten my Steak Diane and was now pouring Coca-Cola down my neck like it was on ration. Mike made several signals for me to 'cool it with eating like a p.i.g.' when Mr Luff wasn't looking, and I eventually calmed down. I now turned my attention to the sweet trolley. This was a transport of delights, featuring a bath-sized trifle made with fresh fruit and topped with glistening, sugar-encrusted strawberries. There was a man-sized chocolate mousse and a gorgeous tarte Tatin. Custards and fresh fruits were also on display, but I only had eyes for the trifle, while Mike and Mr Luff spoke about 'summer seasons' and 'the best setting for Len' and 'the best experience' and 'where he might learn his trade'.

As I finished my meal with perhaps the best trifle known to man, I heard Mr Luff say, 'Yes, definitely – the Minstrels' show in Blackpool next year. Perfect. And he'll do the club tour at the end of this year to get him ready? Excellent. I'll get this.'

He and Mike were shaking hands, and Mr Luff had his beautiful calfskin wallet out and was flipping it open to reveal at least a dozen credit cards. He took out his Diners Club card and laid it on the waiter's little silver tray. He smiled at me and said, 'The Minstrels will be the making of you. The audience aren't there to see the comics; they want to hear all the old songs and look at the costumes. You'll be able to quietly learn your trade.'

And then with a handshake and a shoulder pat he was gone. Mike looked at me and said, 'What a gent,' and that was that. I was booked to play the Black and White Minstrels' club tour at the end of the year and also the summer season the year after. I had no idea what was in store for me, but if I had done a little research, a massive fact would have leapt out at me.

ROBERT LUFF

Robert Luff was the mastermind behind the record-breaking ten-year run of *The Black and White Minstrel Show* at the Victoria Palace Theatre in London. Eight million people crossed the theatre's threshold to watch the long-legged Television Toppers and their blacked-up partners singing songs and occasionally performing a Stephen Foster or Al Jolson medley.

The BBC doesn't like to acknowledge its involvement with the *Minstrel Show* now that it has turned out to be an embarrassment. However, it was a huge success in its day, and was dreamt up by George Inns and George Mitchell, who originally created the show as a one-off. Once broadcast, however, it took the country by storm and became regular Saturday-night fare on BBC1. It also won the Golden Rose of Montreux.

Mr Luff (as I inevitably wound up calling him) was responsible for translating the Minstrels' TV success into a money-making theatrical phenomenon. He rinsed out the format, starting at the Bristol Hippodrome, then took the show on the road for a two-year stint, before settling in at the Victoria Palace in London in 1962.

The most surprising thing in all of this is that I liked him. He was very protective of me and wanted me to learn in a safe environment. From the moment he took me on, I was protected from all the crap that showbiz can throw at you. He had two wonderful women working for him, Gillian and Rhonda. In the absence of a managerial infrastructure, Mr Luff put them in charge of all my bookings and TV work, and they advised and treated me like a grown-up.

Mr Luff told me stories about playing the drums in a dance band. During World War II he was a Gordon Highlander and saw active service in India and Burma. The weight of his experiences, which he never really expanded upon, nevertheless permeated all of our interactions. He would mutter things about being imprisoned, entertaining the troops, the harsh realities of war, and what it meant to be a man of honour in times of cruelty and chaos. I would keep a respectful silence and listen to his stories as carefully as I could, because I knew it cost him something to tell me these things. Strangely, as soon as he'd revealed an interesting nugget about his wartime experiences, he would then clam up and behave as though the information had never been exchanged. Although we had many conversations throughout our association, I felt that I'd only scratched the surface of Mr Luff's past.

In the 1970s he increased his benevolent work and wound up funding medical research and charities. He was a huge supporter of scoliosis and cystic fibrosis charities, and privately funded the department that carried out urinary reconstruction work at the Middlesex Hospital. I think his unending and inspiring efforts to raise money for charity might have had something to do with my later commitment to Comic Relief. Mr Luff was always fundraising, and he urged me to do the same. If there was an event or auction that would be boosted by autograph-signing, Mr Luff insisted I help out. 'The least you can do is give your time,' he would say.

So it was very difficult for anyone to question Robert Luff's integrity or intentions. Whenever I questioned my involvement with the Minstrels, he would talk smoothly about experience and training in show business. He wouldn't get drawn into an argument about race or prejudice; he'd simply sidestep those conversations and insist that his shows were just good old-fashioned entertainment. He really knew his audience: they were a demographic of a certain age, fans of the Great American Songbook and consumers of the old-school musicals of the 1940s and '50s.

When I was in Blackpool in 1976, I would go up to the lighting booth in the gods and watch the shows. No matter how the male cast members presented themselves, there was something fascinating about the audience's love of this kind of spectacle. It was a huge show, full of movement and exotic costumes and popular songs. Mr Luff would come and see us on occasion, like a football manager; he'd just pop in whenever he felt like it to take the temperature of the cast, talk to all the behind-the-scenes staff. I always wanted to put on a good show for him. Despite the embarrassment of being the only real black person among all these fake ones, I still wanted to get out there and make the people laugh.

I had this crazy idea that maybe once he'd realised that I could work any kind of audience, he'd move me out of the Minstrels and put me in some other show. This was not to be. Whenever I talked to Mr Luff about this, he would laugh it off and say that the experience I was getting on the show was indispensable. In many respects he was right – I was playing the biggest performance spaces in the country. However, after the first tour I wanted out and felt that everything I'd gained during my luck-filled run on *New Faces* was draining out of me by the day.

Mr Luff was tough, though. I imagine he wanted me to stay in the show because I was a novelty, and the more I was associated with the show, the more he and his staff could point at me and say, 'How can we be racist? Look – we've got Lenny Henry in the show.' I was vaguely aware that there had been some kind of ruckus with the Race Relations Board. I had become a political football and was being kicked hither and yon. My way through all of this was to bury my head in the sand and let any controversy wash over me.

I managed to get through five years of working with the Black and White Minstrels. Five years of struggling with my identity, learning my craft but also worrying about what my family and friends thought of me and my association with the show. I worked with some lovely people: the Television Toppers were fantastic and friendly to a woman; the Minstrels, underneath all that boot black, were sensitive, hard-working and kind; the four principal performers were always available for chats and advice. Interestingly, whenever they asked Mr Luff for a raise, he would say, 'Well, no one knows who you are under the make-up, so do what you want. I can get someone else.' So they always stayed on, despite feeling undervalued and underpaid.

In the 1980s, when I was no longer represented by Mike Hollis, Mr Luff became my full-time manager. Gillian and Rhonda ran my diary and organised all my dates, while Mr Luff would meet me and talk about overall career issues and offers that had come in. When we dealt with the BBC or ITV, Mr Luff always knew everyone's dad. All the executives we met had massive respect for him. He was someone who had been a part of their parents' lives. He was also incredibly forceful. If he said, 'Maybe there should just be three of them in this show,' the BBC listened. He wasn't scared of putting forward his opinion, and he was rarely wrong. He was also hugely protective of my intellectual property, making sure that I was remunerated for anything I'd invented or made up as part of a team of writers. His belief was that if I'd contributed my energy and improv, then I deserved to get paid too.

Mr Luff may have presided over one of the most mentally bruising periods of my life, but he was also responsible for all my career movements from the end of the 1970s and into the '80s. Whatever he did before that, I have to give him props for his handling of things like *The Lenny Henry Show*, *Lenny Henry Tonite*, *The Delbert Wilkins Show* and Disney's *True*

Identity (1991, dir. Charles Lane). He rocked them like it was no big thing. He taught me a lot about the business and also showed me how to behave in a meeting and when to keep my mouth shut.

When I was in the *New Faces* winners' show at the Palladium, he sent his vintage Rolls-Royce to pick up my mother from Euston Station. Mama sat in the back like an original gangsta, waving at all and sundry and having the time of her life. When I was asked to perform at the Royal Variety Show, Mr Luff once again organised for my mama to be collected in a posh car, but he also managed to fix it so that she could be sat on the same level as the Royal Box. Mama was literally feet away from the Queen. I asked Mama what it had felt like to be that near to her, and she replied that she had waved and offered toffees, but Liz had studiously ignored her. She had a good time anyway.

Mama used to say that Mr Luff cared about people and was a gentleman. I think that's about right.

THE FOSTERS

Shortly after signing with the Black and White Minstrels, I was invited down to London to meet with Michael Grade, who at the time was the deputy controller of programming at London Weekend Television. What I didn't know was that he'd just purchased the 'change of format' rights to an American series called *Good Times*. This was an earthy African American situation comedy set in a housing project in a black inner-city neighbourhood in Chicago. The series was all about a black family's struggles to overcome poverty. LWT intended to create a British version of the show with an Afro-Caribbean cast.

I sat and drank tea, as Grade fiddled with the massive video recorder underneath his TV. I watched an episode called 'Black Jesus' and was captivated by a character called JJ, a lanky, goofy, wise-cracking teenager. I laughed a lot and enjoyed his capering and wordplay. He said things like, 'I am . . . Kid Dyno-mite!' and cracked gags such as, 'I'm gonna make like a tree and leave.' I was still a teenager and thought, 'I think I can do that.' And so I said yes to this new series, which was to be called *The Fosters* – the first all-black situation comedy on British television.

I was invited down to London for rehearsals and to tape the first show in the series, which, to all intents and purposes, was a pilot. (Former *Crackerjack* star and my future mentor Don Maclean would often say that pilot was an acronym for Produced In Little 'Ope of Transmission.)

For the first few days I stayed at the Grosvenor Victoria, a huge hotel near Victoria Station. This was a forbidding place in which you could absolutely lose yourself, a massive block of a building, dirty and imposing. I found myself wandering the floors every night when I got in. Lonely and scared of what was to follow, thoughts kept galloping through my mind. Would I be any good in this show? What did people think of me?

I travelled to work every day by black cab. I was running up a considerable tab but didn't know any better. After four days of rehearsals, I was starting to lose my mind. I was working from ten till six every day, and then returning to my hotel room to learn my lines and take in what I'd been taught that day.

Norman Beaton was playing the dad, Samuel Foster. I had seen him play Nanki-Poo six times in *The Black Mikado* at the Cambridge Theatre in London. He and his co-star Derek Griffiths had me in stitches each time. I loved the way Norman drove the plot with his wordplay and singing. Griffiths was impressively improvisational in his role: if someone arrived late, he'd castigate them from the stage or raise his eyebrows. The crowd would roar their approval.

Once I knew Norman was going to play my dad, I made a point of going round to the stage door to say hi. I was shown up to his dressing room and was greeted by a handwritten note on his mirror in big letters: 'Whoever keeps taking my mother-fucking sunglasses from this room could they leave them where they are!' Really scary.

Despite this, Norman treated me with respect. I'd had no idea who he was before seeing him in *The Black Mikado*, but as the weeks and the rehearsals went by, I realised that he was a bit of a don: he'd sung calypso, he'd been a teacher, he'd acted in Shakespeare's *The Tempest*, he'd helped to establish the Black Theatre of Brixton . . . In short, he was black theatre royalty. I learnt so much just from watching him during rehearsals.

I remember going round to Norman's house one day. He had a statuesque blonde wife and loads of kids. He also had a library containing hundreds of books. He was incredibly generous and would talk to me about culturally significant books like Ralph Ellison's *The Invisible Man* or Alex Haley's *Autobiography of Malcolm X*, and many more. He invited me to come and check him out at the Royal Court in Mustapha Matura's *Playboy of the West Indies*. I was aware of a restlessness within Norman, although I wouldn't dare question him about it. He was fiercely intelligent but also rebellious. He wasn't scared of telling the producer or director off or taking issue with some aspect of the writing. But working with a powerhouse can be testing too. Norman would sometimes show up hungover or still drunk from the night before. This could be irritating, but very funny in retrospect.

The other cast members of *The Fosters* included Canadian-born Isabelle Lucas, who played Pearl Foster, the mum. Isabelle was a lovely, sensitive person with a trilling, almost operatic laugh. She was always incredibly kind to me and helped to steer me through each episode with a quiet authority that I per-haps wasn't aware of at the time. British Guyana-born Carmen Munroe played the sexy next-door neighbour with aplomb and a sharp wit. Carmen also took me under her wing throughout shooting and gave me lots of advice, some of which I took, most of which I ignored. Every so often she would sit me down and read me the riot act: 'Lenny, you're out every night in the clubs, drinking and dancing and carrying on. You should be learning your lines. Why aren't you taking movement and acting and voice lessons? You need training if you're going to survive in this industry.'

Of course, I would just laugh and tease her about being a grumpy grown-up, but she was right. This was the perfect time for an aspirant actor to undertake a period of training, but the trouble was, I was seventeen and in London without parental guidance. Whatever learning I was doing was at the behest of Norman, Isabelle, Carmen and whomever I saw on stage or in the studio. I have no regrets about my time in London making *The Fosters*, but I do know that if I was able to talk to my seventeen-year-old self now, I'd say, 'Yu shoulda listen to Carmen, yu blouse an' skirt eediat!'

There was so much to learn, and I was having to do it all by experience rather than through education, training and reflection. There was a lot of denial going on here. Throughout the entire series I just would not admit how out of my depth I was. This wasn't entirely my fault. There were infrastructural issues that lay at the heart of the show's problems.

We were an Afro-Caribbean family that had its roots in Jamaica, living in Peckham in south-east London. That's what we were meant to be, but Norman and Carmen were from Guyana, Isabelle from Canada, I was from Dudley in the West Midlands, Sharon Rosita (Shirley Foster) was a Barbara Speake-trained, beautifully spoken actress of note, and Lawrie Mark, as my little brother, was a naturally cheeky, funny cockney. We all got on like a house on fire, but it was clear from the moment we appeared on the screen that we were not a real family. We all spoke and behaved differently, there wasn't a coherent family dynamic, but this was the mid-1970s, and although some advances had been made in getting people of colour onto our screens, the executives in charge had no real experience of casting black and brown people. We were all bundled together and basically told to work it out for ourselves. Unless diverse gatekeepers, commissioners and writers are working on a film or television project, you are unlikely to get a truly diverse group of people portrayed accurately on screen or employed gainfully behind the camera. From our vantage point here in the twenty-first century we can observe that there has been some improvement since 1976, but there's still a long, long way to go.

On the basis of the pilot, *The Fosters* was commissioned – thirteen episodes! When it was transmitted, the response was extraordinary. Even though the family were (to my mind) incorrectly cast, even though we were treading in our American predecessor's footsteps, the first episode of the show got 21 million viewers, a figure that remained more or less constant for the rest of the run. The second series was watched by around 10 to 12 million a week – a considerable drop, but you'd kill for those numbers now. We made twenty-seven episodes, the show continuing for two years before running out of steam.

REFLECTION: THE END OF PRIVACY

I often wonder if there is a habitual journey for all children in show business. You've seen these guys on TV, their talent and genius trapped like an exotic bug in a bottle: performers like Mark Lester, Jack Wild, Shirley Temple, Macaulay Culkin – the list goes on and on – all captured at a moment when their precocious, prodigious talents were deemed worthy of adult consumption. Judy Garland, by all accounts, was so in demand in 'little girl' mode that while filming the role of Dorothy in

The Wizard of Oz, the studio executives strapped her breasts down and made her wear a special corset that flattened her curves to make her look younger. Her life as an MGM star was intolerable:

They had us working days and nights on end. They'd give us pills to keep us on our feet long after we were exhausted. Then they'd take us to the studio hospital and knock us out with sleeping pills – Mickey [Rooney] sprawled out on one bed and me on another. Then after four hours they'd wake us up and give us the pep pills again so we could work 72 hours in a row. Half the time we were hanging from the ceiling but it was a way of life for us.
(QUOTED IN 'DARK SIDE OF OZ' BY NEIL NORMAN,
Daily Express, 5 APRIL 2010)

It sounds horrific, and my life from 1975 onwards bears no relation to what Judy Garland and others went through back in the day. But I do sympathise. I was thrust into a completely adult world in which I could sell out a room of club-goers eager to see whether the sixteen-year-old black kid from Dudley could do longer than three minutes. For quite a long time during this period the answer was: no. I probably had a good four minutes in me, but after that things would go terribly wrong. I'm sure many people were surprised at the hodge-podge, higgledy-piggledy, back-of-a-fag-packet, jokes-off-the-telly/from-the-back-of-the-*Beano* nature of my act.

But the blinding glare of publicity and public attention meant that I couldn't go anywhere or do anything without people following me, asking for autographs and reciting my performances back at me. Strangely, I was mostly able to deal with it. I spent a lot of time doing requests for people – impressions of Tommy Cooper, Max Bygraves or Choo Choo from the *Boss Cat* cartoon. I enjoyed the public adulation. I'd never experienced anything like it, and although young and very green, I was determined to squeeze every last morsel from the whole enchilada.

Later, however, sustaining relationships of any kind would become problematic due to interventions by the public. I loved the punters; after all, they had voted for me on *New Faces*. But some of them were very intrusive: just as you were about to snog someone, some hairy-arsed bloke would interject, asking for an autograph, or his girlfriend would ask for a hug, or his mate would ask if I wanted a drink, or two drinks, by which time the person I was trying to snog was invariably snogging someone else.

LIVING WITH JOE CHARLES

In episode one of *The Fosters*, Joseph Charles played a middle-class college professor who was dating my sister, Shirley, while also writing a dissertation entitled 'Sexual Behaviour in the Black Community'. Joe saw that I was having a hard time staying at the Grosvenor Victoria and offered me a bed at his place in Wembley for a very reasonable rate. It was clear to me that it was much better to be living with someone you knew rather than in a large, faceless hotel, where you could die and they might not find you for days. So from that day forward I resided in Wembley.

Joe lived with a lovely woman called Lou, and they both made me feel incredibly welcome in their tiny house on Lancelot Road. I slept on their daybed most of the time. Sometimes I was in the spare room, but for the most part I was under the stairs like Harry Potter, with my belongings – records, cassettes, books – stored underneath the bed.

Joe was a handsome devil, perhaps the best-looking dude I had ever met. He was tall and had abs upon which you could bounce a sixpence. He had trained with the Royal Shakespeare

Company and so had an opinion about everything I did on the stage. In many respects, Joe became a sort of mentor to me just by dint of being around all the time. He'd hear me moaning about work, writers, transport, learning lines, and offer much needed guidance. He was a good guy in a pinch and, as usual, I gravitated towards his paternal nature.

Like most black actors, Joe's employment rate was spotty, to say the least. He would rage about which white actor got what part, and why not him? He was very, very, very funny, but he didn't realise it. Every middle-class twazzock I ever played in a sketch on *Three of a Kind* (1981–3, an award-winning BBC sketch show produced and directed by Paul Jackson) or *The Lenny Henry Show* was usually based on Joe. He was a great person to study. He had a sonorous, resonant, received pronunciation-style voice, but he also had a mockney thing as well. He behaved as though he was a movie star, even when we were walking up Wembley High Street.

Joe would come to the studio to watch *The Fosters* being recorded, and later when I was on *Three of a Kind* he'd come and see that as well. He was a critical friend: if he didn't like a performance, sketch or stand-up bit, he would say so very loudly in the Indian/Greek/Chinese restaurant after the show.

We had many ups and downs, mainly because I wouldn't listen. Joe had a ton of experience of trying to get ahead in the film, TV and theatre industries in the UK and had found every step of the way difficult and strewn with obstacles. Because I was young and always working, I didn't understand what the problem was. I'd ask dumb questions like, 'Why is it so difficult?', 'Why don't you just start your own theatre company?' or 'Why don't you just write and perform your own plays?' Watching Joe get through each day of being out of work was a real lesson. He occasionally worked on a market stall and he cleaned the house a lot. I remember he would smoke certain weird-smelling cigarettes and then embark on an epic amount of hoovering and washing-up and clearing away. He would hector me throughout all of this activity, making me get up and join in, even though I'd arrived at four in the morning after doing Keighley Variety Club or Jollees in Stoke. Joe didn't care, and because I usually slept under the stairs, the incessant vacuuming would wake me up anyway.

THE LOCKSHEN GANG

Joe used to teach drama at a Jewish youth club in north London called Maccabee. When he introduced me to some of his students, I quickly became involved with this new London-based friendship circle. I christened them the Lockshen Gang, after the delicious soup.

Our first meeting was legendary. I had crawled into my below-stairs sleeping station, and at around midnight I was awoken by Joe and a whole bunch of people who immediately began demanding beers, cups of tea, sandwiches and certain magical cigarettes. Soon the place was full of banging and clacking and frying and smoking. I was a bit pissed off at first, but soon began to enjoy the company of his noisy house guests. There was Neil and Jude and Jackie and Jem and Mike and Ian and Lesley and Netty. They were a mostly friendly bunch and invited me to be a part of their group. I grew particularly close to Neil, Jude, Netty and Mike, and began inviting them to studio recordings and shows whenever I was in London. They, in turn, invited me into their homes.

I would sometimes show up and have to wear a yarmulke and sit through prayers in Hebrew, before eating lockshen soup, matzoh bread and a roast chicken dinner. I loved it all. Their families were very amenable and kind. The more I experienced other people's families, the more I began to understand just how unusual mine was. The Lockshen Gang's families were mostly middle class, both parents usually working, educated and living in a relatively large house on a reasonably quiet and affluent street. The grown-ups would include the kids in their conversations; in our family, children were bystanders to whatever the grown-ups were saying or doing.

The Lockshen Gang's parents were incredibly generous – whatever you could eat was yours. I'm sure that is the reason I packed on the pounds during my first two years in show business. I was eating all the time. I'd go to Neil's house, and his mum would say, 'Lenny, have you eaten? Sit, you look starved.' And suddenly I'd be knee deep in matzoh balls – delish!

We talked a lot too, much more than when I was back in Dudley. The gang were my age and they talked about politics, parenting, friendship, sex, drugs, rock 'n' roll, TV, movies, theatre . . . It was exhausting. I was usually the only black guy in the group – or one of two when Joe was there – but I was used to that. I was always treated with respect and love, never ridiculed or rebuffed because I was black. My experience in London was made bearable by my association with the Lockshen posse.

I needed the support too, because this was the year – 1975 – in which I was to embark upon an interminable club tour with the Black and White Minstrels. In the absence of my Dudley friends and family, the Lockshens became my default family. They came to shows, gave me notes and supported me throughout the whole experience.

Who Am I #8

This is a scene from The Fosters *in 1976, the first-ever all-black sitcom to be made in the UK. Norman Beaton is on my right; Rudolph Walker of* Love Thy Neighbour *fame is on my left. This feels like a century ago. Norman and I look like we're in some bizarre multi-generational boy band, while Rudolph looks like he fell in a wardrobe, had a fight, and lost.*

    This was my first-ever acting job, and thank God I got to work with people like Norman and Rudolph. Norman had had huge experience working on stage: he'd been in a calypso band; he'd worked in theatre all over the UK. Rudolph had done loads of telly. I'd been on a talent show for approximately twelve minutes of screen time. Who I am here is 'No-Experience Len'. I'm watching Rudolph like a hawk in case I learn something . . .

6

Minstrelsy

Before we get to the Black and White Minstrels, I want to talk a bit about racism. I saw something in the newspaper recently. It was an article about a gentleman in Devon who'd been arrested because they found explosive devices in his living quarters, plus a diary where he named all the people he hated and wanted to kill, two of whom were my ex-wife, Dawn French, and me. It immediately made me think of a thousand points of dark light, moments when I'd felt shame and embarrassment and rawness because of the colour of my skin.

When I was a kid, I lived next door to a kid called Steven, who was my age and white. He had everything, all the toys you could possibly think of: every single Thunderbird, a Stingray, a Johnny Seven (a silver-painted space rifle, complete with water pistol, red projectiles and glowing lights), a *Man from U.N.C.L.E.* briefcase, a Batman outfit with utility belt, and endless Hot Wheels cars and Dinky toys. Steven was an only child and his parents spared no expense in trying to keep him amused. I'd played with him several times and we got on very well.

One day, something changed. Because we lived so close, Steven would always pop across, knock on the door and ask through the letterbox if I was playing. I would rush to the door, open it, and we'd be off like rockets. But for a few days leading up to this incident, Steven didn't come round. Eventually, I popped over, knocked on his door, opened the letterbox and shouted, 'Steven, you playin'?' There was a silence, and then I saw him approaching the door. He put his lips level with my eyes and then spat and told me not to come round again. I was very young and didn't understand what had changed. Although he didn't say anything racist, it felt as though he'd received some piece of information about who we were and what his behaviour should be when dealing with people like me. It broke my heart. But I carried on with my life, minus Steven.

At Blue Coat secondary modern, there was a massive tectonic shift regarding race, because there were many more people who looked like me. So having been at Jesson's junior school, where I was one of three black kids in the entire student body, I switched to St John's primary and then Blue Coat, where there were many more black and Asian kids. Suddenly, I was having to defend myself not only against white kids, but also against people who looked like me! Talk about a rock and a hard place. This was crazy.

Racism in the park was different. Skinner Williams, a boot-boy type, was always with a gang, and whenever he saw me he took great pleasure in calling me names and insisting that I smelt 'like all nig-nogs do'. He was bigger than me and mobbed up, so I never got the chance to retaliate. I just stood there and took it. Of course, my brother Seymour had the answer: 'Listen, don't let these forkin' eediats get yu down. 'Ear what? I tell yu what yu do. Next time one of these bumba clarts calls yu wog or coon or nig-nog, yu pick up a brick and lick them inna dem neck back.' Although this sounded like a sensible course of action at the time (I was nine), I would eventually eschew this advice. Seymour was on a different journey to me. I was in my h'integration phase. Half killing some kid with a brick would not endear me to polite society.

One Jamaican kid, Mickey Wright, recently arrived from the Caribbean, chased me around Buffery Park with a cricket bat, yelling, 'White man! Yu is a white man!' because he'd heard a Dudley accent when I spoke, and because he'd seen me talking to white kids. He saw this as a betrayal and wanted to beat me to a pulp with the bat. Somehow my fear gave speed to my legs and I ran all the way from the sheds in the park to my front gate, pursued by this kid all the way, and managed to beat him home. For some reason, he didn't walk through the gate, smash down the front door and stalk me through the house. The front door was magic. No non-Henrys allowed, unless invited.

I remember somebody saying to me, in the lead-up to *New Faces*, 'When I say the word "nig-nog", I don't mean you. You're one of us. I mean them other nig-nogs.' I think I just nodded dumbly. Why would somebody say this? Like I was going to reply, 'When I say racist arsehole, I don't mean you. You're like us. I mean the other racist arseholes.' Ignorance is extraordinary.

Perhaps one of the by-products of the H'Integration Project as originated by my mother was that I was denied teeth, having been told to fit in by any means necessary. As a child, fitting in, to my mind, meant: 'Don't rise to any kind of abuse. Ignore it, just get on with it.' Nowadays, I'll speak out against racism and abuse, but I'll do my damnedest not to be drawn into a fist fight.

Sometimes it's difficult to know when people are using racism against you. It could be a slip of the tongue. It could be some act of exclusion. During my time in the Black and White Minstrels I was subjected to little acts of racism almost every day.

In the early days of my marriage to Dawn, a red-top printed a picture of my house on its front page, and as a result the National Front smeared the letters 'NF' on my front door in excrement. They also stuffed burning rags through the letterbox. One guy handwrote messages on tiny squares of paper threatening violence to me and my wife, the pen almost breaking through to the other side he was so angry. He was furious that we were a racially mixed couple and was prepared to do anything to damage our relationship. But we ignored this kind of thing. We knew that there was only a small group of people that had a beef with us regarding our relationship, and we simply chose to ignore them.

However, I do wish I had stood up to racism more. I wonder if turning one's back is really the answer. A lot of my favourite people have refused to allow racism to pollute their lives, and in this age of uncertainty – when *Windrush*-era immigrants are being detained in Yarl's Wood immigration removal centre because they don't possess documentation for every single year of their presence in the UK, or when the residents of Grenfell tower march and march and march in order to draw attention to their predicament, or when anyone who has experienced brutality at the hands of the police during a stop-and-search has been brave enough to talk about it to the media – perhaps it's time to stand up and be counted as far as racism is concerned. Maybe we don't walk away any more. Maybe we stand our ground. As Victoria Wood used to say, 'Whatever they say, just say something back.'

Although I'm rarely on the receiving end of overt racism these days, this might be my way forward. The activists' way. Not seeking out a fight, because I'm shit at fighting. But having lived through riots and insults and people touching my hair on the bus and telling me it's like Velcro, people spitting on their fingers, rubbing my face and saying, 'Ooh look, it doesn't come off,' maybe this is the time to stand up and tell people to back off. Now where does a guy find a half-brick round here?

Who Am I #9

*This is a picture of me in my front room in Douglas Road, when a photographer had come to my house post-*New Faces. *I'm definitely wearing a mask here: it's blackface.*

As the photographer said himself: 'A lovely shot of Lenny Henry when appearing in the Black and White Minstrel Show. *Although he never painted his face for the show, he did this at my request for a publicity shot – it paid off and made the front page.' (*The Black Country Album: 50 Years of Events, People and Places, *Graham Gough, 2012)*

DON MACLEAN

In 1975 I went to the Exhibition Centre on Broad Street in Birmingham. Robert Luff had suggested that I go and meet Don Maclean, who was in residency at the time. Don was a stalwart of children's TV – he was a presenter on the BBC's *Crackerjack!* – and he was also the compère and resident comedian on the TV version of *The Black and White Minstrel Show*. He would resume his *Minstrel Show* compèring duties in 1976 at the Blackpool Opera House.

Don was doing two performances a day at the Exhibition Centre. He was working with Jan Hunt, a vivacious comedy performer and singer. They did a double act to begin the show:

Jan: 'What's good for women's rights?'

Don: 'Men's lefts!'

Jan would do a very professional solo set, and then Don would do his comedy act to finish. He was absolute dynamite. This was the first time I'd seen a proper professional comic up close and personal. Here I was able to watch how Don worked the room. He was like radar, slowly taking in every single angle, smiling continually and dropping joke bombs like they were going out of style. He had a Jerry Lewis-like appeal to me – lanky, goofy, silly, gurning. He did whatever it took to get the joke over the line. It was a *big* performance. Don had a powerful singing and speaking voice and an effortless delivery. From the minute I saw him I knew that I had to be more like him and less like me. This was the mimic in me hard at work. 'Whatever you do, Len, don't be yourself – that's not good enough. You've got to be like *him*.'

This was the beginning of an obsession for me: how could I get to a place where *I* was slaying the crowd every night? I made it my business to watch Don perform several times that week, and what I noticed was his consistency. His show was predictable, in that he always got the laughs to come where they were supposed to be. Every. Single. Time. It was amazing to watch. He would stalk the stage like a velociraptor, marking out his territory and spraying jokes out to each point of the compass. He'd walk on stage and just hammer us with jokes, and it built and built and built till he got to the climax. The final sequence of patter would reduce the audience to tears of laughter.

When I did the Exhibition Centre shortly after, I was embarrassingly inadequate. I did everything I'd done in my *New Faces* performances, but it was very disorganised. I had my props and my table and my music, but it was very amateurish. I was lost. I used to have one of those laughing bags from a joke shop. You pressed a button and maniacal laughter would issue forth from the bag. I took that on stage with me and pushed the button every time there was an absence of laughter. I pushed it a lot during my residency.

Who Am I #10

*This is me and Don in about 1976. I don't know where we are.
It looks like Blackpool. Don did a very good job with me, as a
mentor. He took me under his wing and taught me the basic
tenets of showbiz etiquette: always press your suit before you go
on; no need to wash your shirt after a first house, but good idea
to hang it over a radiator; don't shout into the microphone, it's
already making your voice louder; make a point of addressing
the right and left sides of the audience and look up sometimes –
those bastards have paid good money to see the show.*

    *Don welcomed me into his family at a time when my own
family were physically distant and couldn't help me even if they
wanted to. This was a transition period of sorts. The* New Faces
*experience was becoming just a memory. I was moving into
Minstrel territory now and I needed a spiritual guide of sorts.*

Don took the helm like a champ and dragged me, kicking and screaming, into the realm of professional performance.

Don was married to the lovely Toni, with two kids, Rory and Rachel. They made me feel as though I was part of the family, and understood innately what problems I might be going through at this stage. I don't think the whole Black and White Minstrels thing had sunk in yet, which is why I look like I'm having such a good time. My relationship with Don would be a springboard to the next phase of my career. I owe him a lot. I hero-worshipped him and copied everything he did performance-wise in a strange, obsessive way for the longest time. Later, this obsession would get me into trouble.

THE CLUB TOUR 1975–6

The Minstrels' club tour at the end of 1975 was a massive opportunity for me to learn, and despite all the attendant ethical and moral issues surrounding my involvement, I took it. I had no idea what I was letting myself in for until, at the press call, I was positioned between two blacked-up dancers, given a sparkly hat and told to pretend that 'I was a minstrel too'. It finally sank in: this was going to be tough.

The tour proceeded from just before Christmas and into 1976, as we ground our way through Jollees in Stoke, Batley Variety Club, Caesar's Palace, Luton, and the Showboat Theatre in Cardiff. There were more, but my memory has blotted them out. Beforehand there was an extensive rehearsal period with a full orchestra. I had my music written out by a lovely guy called Colin Campbell, who lived in the Midlands. He wrote out a complete set of 'dots' for me – intro to Dave Allen, intro to Kojak, intro to Frank Spencer, etc., plus stings for each ending.

Don Maclean had sat down with me and gone through my twelve-minute first-half spot. He was brutal. Nothing was good enough and he made me work over and over again on timing, delivery and content. I practised continually, and when the time came I gave it my best shot and (in my mind anyway) managed to get away with it. I was on really early in the show – the second spot in part one – so I had time to watch the other performers. The Minstrel boys were all capable of singing and dancing simultaneously, but they were never required to. All their numbers had been professionally recorded and arranged in London. There were two sets of Grundig tape machines running continually throughout the show, and the tapes contained lead and backing vocals, plus live-sounding 'taps' for when Les

Want, one of the main performers, did his American Songbook/ Fred Astaire-style routine.

In my experience, the tape only malfunctioned once – at Blackpool during summer season in 1976. The Minstrels were up there, 'singing' and dancing their hearts out, perfect, multi-layered Brian Wilson-style harmonies, and then – SNAP! – the tape broke and we were left with the half-mumbled moans and groans of people who'd never expected to be singing live. The audience's reaction was a mixture of shock, awe and revulsion. I pissed myself laughing.

Backstage I got on really well with the guys and girls. The boys were mostly slightly older than me, some of them straight, quite a few of them gay. I'd never encountered this many gay men before, but everyone's gung-ho good-naturedness meant I was able to overcome my provincial naivety. They were fun off stage and looked after me when I needed it. I was igno-rant about such matters, but eventually I was to learn that as long as you minded your beeswax and were sensitive, then you were cool.

Our first date on the tour was at Caesar's Palace, Luton, a massive nightclub that held over a thousand people. The show had sold out weeks before, and the place was packed out for seven nights. I've never seen a show in a club like it before or since. The Minstrels rolled with a full theatre crew, lighting, sound, sets and stage management. There was a twenty-piece orchestra in the pit, plus ten boys, ten girls, four principals, two comics and two speciality acts. The show was drilled to per-fection; even I felt a responsibility to do my best and deliver the goods. I had managed to string together, with Don's help, a decent twelve-minute set. I used music to link the whole thing and at one point utilised special effects: strobe lighting in order to imitate Steve Austin, the six-million-dollar man. During all of this, I felt very much at the mercy of each audience I faced: if they liked me, then I'd have a good show; if they took a dislike to me, then I'd have a shit one. It never occurred to me that it was always within my gift to make it a positive or negative experience. It's never the audience; it's always you.

So this was my job from the end of 1975 into 1976 – the Minstrels' club tour. We schlepped all over England. I really liked almost everyone in the show, and I'm pretty sure I was in love with nearly all the dancers at some point or other. I was a hormonal teenager with spots and enthusiasm in abundance. The social side of things was great. We'd go out for curries, Chinese food and fish and chips. We'd have parties and dance till we dropped. However, all our youthful moxie and attitude would drop off us in chunks once we got to the stage door of the club or theatre and were reabsorbed into this odd institution that demanded that its male performers wore shoe black on their faces and the women fishnets, high heels and feathers.

It was a show steeped in vaudeville and music hall; the jokes were old, but the songs were older. The principal singers sang anything, from the Great American Songbook to light opera; from musical westerns to middle-of-the-road fare from the days before rock 'n' roll. Les Want was a fantastic performer and would perform a show-stopping sequence in the style of Al Jolson, Jimmy Cagney or Gene Kelly that would bring the house down every night. I used to sit in his dressing room some nights, and he'd tell me about his days in the business. Although I was just a kid, he was incredibly frank about things. He didn't really dig being in a minstrel show, but it paid the bills. He wished he was paid more for what he was doing but realised that – as Mr Luff had pointed out – because he was blacked up all the time, no one knew who he was and therefore his currency as a performer was diminished. I never saw him work at his performances; he told me this was all stuff he knew through instinct and from previous shows.

The Television Toppers were a group of young female dancers who had either been in the show before or had been recently cast from other troupes, such as the Second Generation. They were all pretty much in their late teens/early twenties and were treating this tour and subsequent shows as an adventure or rite of passage. They seemed incredibly grown up to me, smoking and drinking shorts with mixers. You couldn't get near them, which was probably for the best. One of my friends in the male minstrels was a boisterous and funny Liverpudlian called Pete. He'd fallen in love with a statuesque dancer called Penny. After a few weeks, he became frustrated by her inability to commit and wound up putting his fist through a window at a party. All boisterousness and amusement melted away like a '99' ice cream during a heatwave.

Don continued to give me advice throughout this period, and I somehow managed to get through without too much egg on my face. Being in the Minstrels was an issue, though. I noticed that my family didn't talk about it much. Seymour stayed out of the way, and Kay didn't have much to say about it either. I wasn't a pariah, but no one spoke about it when I went home. What had I done?

REFLECTION: WHY IS EVERYONE SO UNHAPPY?

I don't know if it struck me then, but in retrospect very few of the adult entertainers whom I was trying to mirror on stage seemed happy. They all arrived at venues with their game face on – a tough veneer of 'Don't fuck with me' that only softened once they knew they could trust you or realised that you could actually do your job. Nobody was impressed by the fact that I'd won *New Faces*. They all seemed to treat TV talent shows with disdain: 'They're all fixed. If you're prepared to shag Hughie Green, you could be on *Opportunity Knocks* for weeks.'

There was a frustration that pervaded the atmosphere backstage. Soundchecks were fraught with braggadocio, mainly from the male acts. 'I stormed it last night, I annihilated 'em.' 'Well, I murdered 'em. I tore the bollocks off 'em!' This didn't feel like entertainment to me; it was more like a kind of torture. I would often sit on my own and wonder what it would be like to be in an audience and have a comedian come on and attempt to rip off your testicles. As a seventeen-year-old it all felt a bit transgressive, weird, alien. But I used to nod and smile and laugh as if I knew what they were talking about. It would be years before I understood what they actually meant: just that they'd put on a good show and the audience had laughed a lot.

Staying in digs was interesting because you'd see a lot of these people off duty, at breakfast, in a jumper and pants, eating beans on toast, drinking endless cups of tea, talking about doing three shows the night before, dying on their arse at two of them, getting a stander at the last one and being paid in readies in the car park. Older performers – guitar vocalists, impressionists, comedians, instrumentalists and magicians – were akin to vagabonds, mountebanks and felons, constantly moving from town to town, wreaking havoc and then skipping town before daybreak to avoid hostile landlords or irate husbands.

I regularly shared dressing rooms with odd combinations of performers – usually a comedian, a girl singer and a speciality act. The comedian would nearly always be trying to get off with the girl singer. The speciality act would be practising constantly. Because of my *New Faces* status, I would normally be top of the bill. The comedian, usually a white bloke of a certain age, would almost always be pissed off with this and would slip in some disparaging or racist remark. This was a tough experience for a young kid, difficult to overcome. Actually, I'm not sure I ever have overcome it, even now.

I met a lot of forty-something comics who were either about to be or had just been divorced, or were just about to embark on their second or third marriage. Of course, there were the guys who were happily married or in stable relationships, but truth be told, this was the 1970s, and most guys in the business chased women relentlessly and made no bones about it. As a young single guy, I found this incredibly confusing. I was a teenager, and I felt I was permitted to have adolescent crushes and go all googly-eyed and soppy whenever I was at a disco or enjoying post-show drinks. I didn't expect to see grown-ups behaving in the same way too.

But it was fun. There was a sense of 'what happens on the road, stays on the road'. This wayward behaviour became a topsy-turvy norm that would prove problematic in later years. It certainly didn't lead to happiness, and in retrospect I feel sorry for a lot of the older comedians I met. And I feel sorry for myself. There's a strong argument that says a teenage boy shouldn't have been allowed into this deeply confused and transgressive world unchaperoned. Why was no one watching out for me? Mike Hollis would pop in sometimes and attend certain shows, but he was a ghostly presence. It became clear to me that I would have to seek that mentorship elsewhere or else sink slowly to the bottom, never to return to the surface. That was one thing about the older acts: all of them were prepared to dispense pearls of wisdom, and I would listen hard – and it was hard to take sometimes:

'You're a good lad, you've got a lot of potential, but you're unseasoned.'

'You're not that funny, but you've got something.'

'Look, lad, there's no sense being miserable. You were shite tonight, you'll be shite tomorrow and, lookin' at yer act, you're gonna be shite for a few years to come. But it's gonna get better, trust me.'

I took this to heart. Club audiences were a tough crowd, every performance a battlefield. Authority had to be established immediately or they would steamroller you, and that was you done. Opening with appropriate jokes was essential, otherwise you'd just get murdered, shamed or humiliated, and all because you didn't have the right opening gags. I used to say:

'Good evening. Enoch Powell says he wants to give me a thousand pounds to go back where I came from. Which is great, because it's only twenty pence for me to get on the bus from here to Dudley.'

I used to open with 'That Old Black Magic', singing the first two lines and then saying, 'Black magic – that's got to be me doing Tommy Cooper.' And then, as Tommy, 'I walked into a bar. I said, "Ouch." It was an iron bar. A skeleton walked in behind me and said, "Can I have a pint of bitter, please, and a mop?"'

Sometimes I'd be in Charlie Williams mode: 'You'd better laugh, or I'll come and move in next door to you. That'll bring your rent down.'

I toggled between several openings over the first few years. And I don't think I was happy with any of them. In those early days, for me there was a sense of 'Just get on, just get on, just get on.' I knew that somewhere there'd be something that they'd laugh at, because they'd laughed on telly. And if they'd liked that kid who'd done the impressions, well, I was going to do those impressions now.

I struggled a lot during this period, but the great constant was my enjoyment of actually being on stage. That never went away. It was just the content that was the problem. But as I travelled around, watching these older comics and learning all their tricks, the experience I gained from performing in working men's clubs, military bases, leisure centres and broken-down cinemas started to accrue. The more hours I put in, the better I got. But only in the sense of survival. The first five or six years in the business were all about scrabbling to the shore without being eaten by the sharks. It wasn't about being excellent or thinking carefully about ideas, surprises, narrative, musical interpolations and characterisations. All of that would come much, much later. In the meantime, I was swimming with the grumpy comedians, speciality acts and girl singers, and kind of enjoying it, in a miserable sort of way.

MORE MINSTRELS AND KEN DODD

Once the Minstrels' club tour was over, I was back in London prepping for the first series of *The Fosters*. But later in 1976 I was booked once more for the Minstrels in Blackpool. This part of my journey was difficult. From the end of 1975 to 1981 I was contractually obliged to appear in the Minstrels' show. Six years of 'Oh, Dem Golden Slippers', 'Paddlin' Madelin' Home' and 'Ballin' the Jack'. Apart from short interludes in pantomime, clubland and Felixstowe (in the John Hanson summer show, where no one wore black shoe polish on their faces) my life now was one of creeping dread.

From this point on the Minstrels scenario was, for the most part, a duvet of sadness. I was not forced to wear blackface like the late-nineteenth/early-twentieth-century minstrel acts in the US. Bert Williams was one such performer. He wore blackface at a time when his African American audience was questioning why anyone would choose to do so.

I was fortunate not to have to wear shoe polish on my face. I only ever had to do my twelve-minute act in the first half of the show. But I was in a strangely split mental condition for most of the time. On the one hand, I was working with the loveliest of people: the dancers, the singers and the crew were very kind and nurturing. On the other, I was a seventeen-year-old black guy performing in a minstrel show for what seemed like forever. Having begun my journey so triumphantly, I was suddenly in the doldrums, adrift, lost. I would arrive at the theatre and know that I would be the only black person in the building, perhaps the only black person within a fifty-mile radius. The dislocation I felt as I walked out, looked at the audience and saw no one who looked like me was palpable. But somehow I managed to supress these feelings. After all, I was contributing to my mother's house-keeping bills, and I would eventually buy her a house, a phone, a colour TV and the rest. I was told that my responsibility was to use this wonderful opportunity to improve as a performer. The whole thing stretched out in front of me like Plastic Man and Reed Richards of the Fantastic Four having a tug-of-war.

I took to staying in bed for most of the day, leaving my digs at four to get to the theatre in time for the half-hour call. I overate, gained weight, then desperately embarked on an insane bout of keep-fit activity. I was down, way, way down, and only a change would break the spell. There were moments when I wished my brothers, Seymour and Hylton, would smash down the doors and come and rescue me from yet another interminable summer season. It never happened.

C. S. Lewis said:

Mental pain is less dramatic than physical pain, but it is more common and also more hard to bear. The frequent attempt to conceal mental pain increases the burden: it is easier to say 'My tooth is aching' than to say 'My heart is broken.'

I think the most painful aspect is the fear of ridicule, job loss, failure. I was a teenager when all this was happening to me. But I had to stick at it, no matter what.

Because I was away from Greg and Mac – and the Lockshen Gang as well – I was isolated. I had to make new friends all the time. I could do that, but it wasn't the same as having a consistent circle of friends. I had no entourage living with me, nurturing and supporting me. It was just me.

There was a major event during the season at Blackpool that taught me a lesson I will never forget. Don Maclean was doing a sterling job of warming the audience up, compèring and finally delivering a killer set at the end that left the punters happy and geared up for the big finale. I watched his performances every night and knew every line off by heart. One Friday night at teatime we got the message that Don would not be coming in to do the show because his father-in-law was gravely ill. Don said, 'Len will stand in for me till I get back.' I was told this as I walked in at 5.30 p.m. for the first show. This was a shock to me – especially as I had only twenty minutes of stage-ready material. What was I going to do?

Here's what I did: I went on and opened the show as I'd seen Don do over two hundred times. I then went on and closed part one, as I'd seen Don do, and finally I slammed them at the end. I got big laughs and many applause breaks. At the end of it all I noticed that the backstage staff, and the stage managers in particular, were ashen-faced as I left the stage. What had I done wrong? Well . . . it turns out that when you're asked to fill in for someone, they don't mean for you to use their material. My mimicry gene had kicked in and I'd repeated, parrot fashion, all the pieces that I had taken in from watching Don over and over again.

When I arrived the next day I was stood down by the stage manager, who had contacted Keith Harris to come and stand in for Don while he was away on compassionate leave. I was told very firmly that you don't do what I had done. You use your own material at all times. I hung my head for two weeks, until people started telling me how well I'd done.

Keith, on the other hand, was a revelation. He was a slick

ventriloquist; he wore all the hip gear – tight trousers and bolero jackets – and had a mullet haircut (later a bubble perm). He was full-on show business: he knew all the dance steps, the silly voices, the gags, the tricks. When he stood in for Don, he marmalised the audiences.

One of the upsides of the summer season experience was you got to meet everyone, whether you wanted to or not. I saw Ken Dodd perform one Sunday at the Blackpool Opera House. He came on in a big red furry coat, with a ten-foot tickling stick, accompanied by his theme music, 'Love Is Like a Violin'. He riffed and joked and gagged us for forty minutes, then introduced someone else and disappeared. Someone sang. We all went to the loo. Doddy came back and did another forty-five minutes. He had a big bass drum, which he said was useful for telling the time if you don't have a watch because when you pummel it late at night, people always stick their head out of the upstairs window and say, 'Who's playing the drums at four o'clock in the bloody morning?'

When I looked around the audience I recognised lots of young comics dotted around, all of them with a notepad and pencil, trying to write down whatever they could. One of the gags that went round the circuit was about a young comic wishing he'd shouted out, 'Could you slow down, Doddy? I've dropped me pencil.'

I always imagined Ken Dodd's brain to be like a huge library full of jokes, with a custodian on roller skates zooming from subject to subject, locating the correct joke for each moment and plugging one into Doddy every forty-five seconds. It certainly felt that the maestro plied his craft so expertly that there was no way he could fail on stage. He had a ton of jokes – and the delivery to match. There was a point in the show, about two and a half hours in, when he looked at us, making that buck-toothed face, and said:

'D'you give in?'

And then:

'If, in a minute, a bunch of soaked, angry people come in and sit on your laps, don't worry – it's just the second house!'

Then he did another hour.

What I didn't know was that Doddy worked with writers. Eddie Braben, who went on to work for Morecambe and Wise and many others, was one of those who grafted and worked and stressed and strained to produce the mountain of material that someone of Doddy's stature required on a monthly basis – routines, patter, one-liners, musical numbers. Doddy did them all and demanded the highest of standards.

The northern comedian Nicky Martyn was a huge fan, and I think Victoria Wood was too – I always noticed that she held her fingers aloft in a similar way to Doddy. I found out that he used to write jokes on his fingers – fingers as autocue. It works. When I met Doddy backstage, he always talked about the burden of being top of the bill and how the management only came in when the theatre wasn't full. Then he'd offer you a brown ale and, half joking, tell you, 'That'll be three and sixpence, sir . . .'

Then, suddenly, my first Black and White Minstrels summer season at the Blackpool Opera House was over. The performers and backstage crew had been my family for that entire summer. Apart from the drudgery of performing for twelve minutes and then having to twiddle my thumbs for the rest of the night, the actual experience of being away from home (again) for a whole summer had been a process of maturation for me. I had lived through thirteen episodes of a situation comedy with Norman Beaton and co., and then endured a summer season in Blackpool without killing my career – or myself.

In the autumn of 1976 I was back in the working men's clubs and doing the odd TV performance, earning my living from show business, but all that energy, all that excitement at being halfway decent at something, all that stardust and glitter was as nothing until I could establish who I was. If I was going to survive in this industry, something had to happen in order for me to achieve the potential promised by my initial appearance.

I crossed my eyes, fingers and toes and . . . jumped.

Who Am I #11

So here I am. I'd just had this oddly mixed experience of being in a hugely successful show with the Black and White Minstrels. This palette of conflicting emotions was something I would carry around with me until at least 1980.

Leading into 1977, I was strangely buoyant, but there was more professional angst to follow. (Shutterstock)

SUMMER SEASON 1977

I worked the 1977 summer season at the Spa Pavilion in Felixstowe with matinee idol John Hanson. In my youthful ignorance, I had no idea that Hanson had made an album of *The Vagabond King/ The Student Prince* that went to number 9 in the UK charts. I didn't know that he had played the Red Shadow in a record-breaking production of *The Desert Song* at the Palace Theatre in London in 1967. I had seen him on *The Morecambe and Wise Show*. Eric and Ernie had teased him something rotten about *The Desert Song*, and I remember my family killing themselves laughing, even though none of us knew anything about him.

Hanson was approximately fifty-five years old when I worked with him, still handsome and fit, his face artfully made up with fake tan and just a little eyeliner – and the blackest hair I'd ever seen. He was every inch the middle-aged matinee idol and had a fervent following among the blue-rinse brigade. In fact, whenever he left the stage door, he'd be mobbed by women of a certain age. I didn't envy him.

He carried himself like the star he was and remained relatively isolated throughout the entire twelve-week run. He could belt out a song, though. Having been a boy soprano when he was younger, he now fitted into the Howard Keel style of singing – full-blooded and right in the sweet spot. He would occasionally clear his throat of phlegm mid-number during the instrumental bits – a massive hawk and then a loud swallow. The audience never heard, but everyone backstage was like, 'Daaaaayumn! That one must have had bones in it!'

Peter Butterworth was second on the bill. He'd chat to me in the breaks during rehearsals about his long career acting in sketches with Terry-Thomas and playing minor roles in films alongside everyone from Douglas Fairbanks Jr to Sean Connery.

Peter and I had worked together previously in pantomime in Bournemouth, so there was a familiarity there that I didn't have with Hanson.

Also on the bill was a magic act called Anna and Maria, two glamorous, sequin-wearing ladies who presented illusions in a choreographed manner. They had a massive parrot called Miggsy, who would say things from the wings during the performance. At the time, I had the dressing room nearest the stage. I would play loud music on my boombox and dance and move until I had to go on. It was a ritual. (The eighteen-minute live version of 'Pick Up the Pieces' by the Average White Band was a particular favourite at the time.) Then I'd make my way to the side of the stage and wait in the wings. Every night I'd be in the queue with Anna and Maria and Miggsy, who was not a big fan of John Hanson. Once while I was waiting to go on Miggsy started to mimic Hanson's singing, but in an out-of-tune, high-pitched squawk. It was very loud and distracting. Hanson was on stage trying to sing, but looking off to the side as if to say, 'What the hell's going on?'

He stormed off stage, saw me waiting to go on and said, 'Mr Henry, I want a word when you've finished.' I went on and did my thing, and then went to his dressing room. On entering, I was surrounded by the aromas of eucalyptus and peppermint coming out of steaming bowls, photographs of his family, the works, everything for the professional singer in residence. His dressing room was very neat indeed. I felt slightly ashamed of my chaotic, Fungus the Bogeyman-style cave, which was mostly dominated by my boombox, a heap of dirty stage-wear and half a ton of cassettes. There was a meaningful silence before Hanson drew my attention to the order of the day: Lenny Henry mocking John Hanson's singing mid-show. I swore blind on my mother's grave that it was the parrot, but he just shouted at me to get out. I was ashamed that he didn't believe me, and it cast a pall over the next few weeks.

However, one thing happened to cheer me up. After a month, the management at the Spa Pavilion reported back to the promoters that Peter Butterworth's act was a bit thin. I loved Peter, but I had no idea what he was up to out there. He wasn't really a stand-up and was doing a rather camp, rambling, characterful chat, which wasn't going down particularly well with the punters. So the promoter called and told me that I would now finish the first half of the show, that I could do twenty minutes instead of fifteen. I was ecstatic – this was the first time my talents had been acknowledged like this, a moment akin to a battlefield promotion. Peter was very kind about it. He supported me throughout the whole transition process and made me feel fit to take over his position. He was a true gentleman and never held this change in the hierarchy against me.

But there were other things to be dealing with during this summer season.

I had met a drummer called Martin, who played with a band called the Amazing Bavarian Stompers. They were playing at a nearby *Biergarten* and had garnered a considerable following. Martin and I had met at a local benefit, immediately becoming soulmates. We had a mutual love of Richard Pryor, Bill Cosby and funk music. We listened to music together and I got him into the Ohio Players and the up-the-country thumpin' Bootsy Collins. He played me tapes of *The Goon Show* and insisted that I like them. I did enjoy the Goons, but when I bought the script books I was alarmed to discover dodgy stage directions in the margins, such as '3 coons sing during this bit'. I liked the madness of the writing, all the catchphrases, the silly voices. This madcap style came out of Spike Milligan's time in the army – that get-up-and-go, anything goes style of ENSA entertainment. The jokes and catchphrases came thick and fast, with a surrealist backdrop. I enjoyed all that stuff, but I did *not* enjoy the casual racism.

Martin and I used to eat at a café run by a sandy-haired, bespec-tacled guy called Reg. The café was away from the seafront and down a side street. It served *massive* English breakfasts and Sunday roast-type meals. I was in heaven. This was the closest I'd been to Henry-style portions since I'd left home. Martin, being a drum-mer and from Halifax, would order two of everything and then gobble down the whole lot, washing it down with gallon mugs of tea. In my stupidity, I would try to match him spoonful for spoonful. It wasn't a competition, but there I was, trying to keep up with a maniacal drummer who burnt several thousand calories every performance. Martin's big trick after each meal would be to say, 'That were lovely. Can I have the same again, Reg?' And I would say the same. Something had to give – and it did.

For my sins I had agreed to perform in the Stevie Wonder medley that opened the second half of the show: 'You Are the Sunshine of My Life', 'My Cherie Amour' and 'Isn't She Lovely' – definitely the non-funky side of Stevie's work. We had to wear Second Generation-style outfits during this routine. I was in a white catsuit with pink, purple and orange panels, with tassels hanging from each sleeve. I looked ridiculous. The fit on the costume was relatively snug, as you can't really wear a baggy catsuit for a dance number – I would have looked like a plumber who'd wandered on stage from the car park.

About five weeks into the season, I'm in the middle of the dance break of 'Isn't She Lovely' when I notice that the seams of my pants are giving way at the back. I try to minimise my movements, but it's too late. Sixteen bars later, I do a pirouette and my pants split from backbone to navel. I had put on so much weight that the costume was no longer fit for purpose. Thankfully, I habitually wore underwear, otherwise this would have been a different kind of performance . . .

Martin, being a musician and therefore perhaps more pro-active, behaved in a ruthless fashion when it came to courting members of the opposite sex. I was still relatively young and any snogging etc. that would occur would usually be because Martin had begun the conversation. Back in Dudley my MO was to show off for Greg, Mac and the rest of the lads and hope that some girl was watching me act the fool. Then, when something slow came on, like 'Summer Breeze' by the Isley Brothers or 'My Girl' by the Temptations, I'd ease across and ask her if she wanted to dance.

In 1977 I was nineteen and assumed to be a bit of a playa, but really I wasn't. I was finding it increasingly difficult to maintain the charade of being Barry White from the Black Country. I was hopeless with girls, and it was becoming an embarrassment. I think my main technique was to go wherever the object of my desire was that day and make eyes at her. It was like Puss in Boots from *Shrek*, when he's doing the huge eyes routine. Martin was very blunt with the ladies, no messing around: 'Are you interested, love? Otherwise I've got a pie in the oven.' He was a charmer.

BACK IN LONDON, 1977

After Felixstowe there was a brief sojourn back in Dudley. I was restless, out of sorts. My family didn't know what to do with me. I was no longer the kid from Dudley, and there was no real connection with my former school mates. Greg, Mac and Tom – the Grazebrook Crew – were away, following their own paths. I was isolated, a road runner, never staying in one place too long. In many respects, I was glad to get on the road again.

1977 was another year of *The Fosters* for me. Also, London had become less of a mystery due to my friendships with Joe and Neil, Jude, Netty and the rest. We went to see shows like *Bubbling Brown Sugar*, with the delightful Helen Gelzer and a spectacular cast, all choreographed by the mighty Charles

Augins. We saw the film of the *Rocky Horror Picture Show* about six times! Of course, the clubbing, partying and carousing carried on apace too. I also got to know Norman Beaton a bit better around this time. He would show up at Gulliver's nightclub and, like a character from an old Peter Sellers routine, would ask at reception if it was possible to cash a cheque. I used to mimic Norman for the bouncers. I'd come in, hopping on both feet, and the guys on the door would say:

'What's going on with you?'

And I'd reply:

'I've got one of Norman's cheques in my pocket!'

I don't know why Norman was broke, because he always seemed to be working. He was appearing in a film called *Black Joy* (1977), which was chosen by the Cannes Film Festival and won favourable reviews at home and abroad. He was also about to work on *Black Christmas*, directed by Stephen Frears, which would eventually lead to his starring role in the UK's first black soap opera, *Empire Road* (1978–9), so it was all happening for Norman. But he was constantly broke and partying a lot, while teaching me how to act as the eldest son in *The Fosters*.

Meanwhile, I was still sleeping under the stairs at Joe's house, and I was beginning to notice a pattern. When Joe was working, everything was cool under the sun. But when he was out of work and having to hustle for a few quid here and there, he would stomp around the house hoovering with a big black cloud over his head. He would roll up one of his curious cigarettes, watch television and moan about the lack of opportunities for actors of colour. Here was a constant reminder of how lucky I was. Even though Joe had been in episode one of *The Fosters*, he hadn't been asked back. He was now plying his trade at the Royal Court or the National Theatre or wherever, whenever possible. It was a tough existence for him, whereas I would just schlep to Workington or Dorset or Cardiff, do a working men's club or one of the bigger venues, and then come home, having made enough money to pay the bills for the next few months. Eric and Ernie used to call the big club gigs 'bank raids', and they were right to some extent. Club comics could earn a decent living, even the ones who'd never really done a lot of telly. As long as they'd made an appearance on a show like *Sunday Night at the London Palladium* or *Seaside Special*, they managed very well.

I think it might have been Joe's plight that kept me from taking on a theatre role for as long as I did. I saw that he wasn't happy, that the gaps between jobs were huge, and that when he did work, he moaned all the way through about the money, the hours, sharing a dressing room . . . Being an actor, he was out of work for quite lengthy stretches of time. His response to working actors on the telly was hilarious: he would really slag them off. He just didn't seem to like anybody. His comments were cutting:

'Couldn't act his way out of a wet paper bag.'

'Yeah, *that's funny* . . . NOT! Dickhead thinks he's a comic but couldn't time a joke if he had a Timex jammed up his arse!'

Sometimes he'd just yell at the TV, 'NOT GOOD ACTING!'

There was a brief moment when Joe and I were on our own in the house for various reasons – a change in relationship status is perhaps the best way of putting it. When single, Joe became incredibly strict around the house: he hated it if you left the toilet seat up or if you didn't hoover at least once a week. I would put music on, sing along and get on with it. Joe would hoover with a vengeance, cursing anyone who had allowed biscuit crumbs to besmirch his carpet. I'm sure the inhalation of certain substances had a lot to do with this rage. Rather than calm Joe down, they seemed to have the opposite effect. He didn't chill; he would heat up and become more and more furious. It was scary sometimes, and I tended to back down at those moments.

Generally, he would have my back when we were out and about of an evening. He always stood his round and was smooth with any lady who strolled across our path. Joe didn't do the traditional chat-up lines; it was more the way he stood, making sure the light hit him in a certain way. I would just pray that her boyfriend didn't hit him first.

He was always fair about my staying at his house. He replaced lost keys, drove me to gigs on occasion and cooked many, many meals for me. He was a mensch for most of the time. Although later in my career there were occasions when we didn't get on, at this point in my life we were getting on fine.

REFLECTION: MIMICRY IS SURVIVAL

The experience of working on *The Fosters* was perhaps a portent of things to come. Here I was, playing someone *my own age*. The scripts were funny, and there was a recognisable structure to the work. This was clearly the gods giving me a sign: 'Be an actor, Len! Somebody else writes a script, and then a director tells you how to do it. You don't have to drive to Middlesbrough and do Charlie Williams's jokes. It's all written for you.'

I loved being a young man playing a young man, and being on the scene in 'the Smoke' at a time when there were great clubs and even greater music. It took my mind off the day job, the constant grind of working the clubs and trying to figure out just exactly what I was doing up there. Perhaps I should have taken up the challenge and accepted more acting work earlier, but it just didn't occur to me. Once I committed to learning the art of being a stand-up comedian/impressionist/entertainer, I pretty much stayed the course for twenty years, with the odd foray into acting, but never to the point of distraction. These were hard lessons to learn, and it's interesting looking at old photographs of myself during this period, because you can see me trying on different faces – a plethora of masks. 'Which one do I like? This one? How about this one?'

I would grow tired of this ingratiating mimicry. But not for a while. I was fast learning how to present a moving target. If you get stuck in a trench, it becomes your grave, so I kept changing what I did, because nothing was working. The act of creativity, of trying to reinvent yourself, is painful. I was constantly remaking and remodelling my identity; constantly hurtling off a cliff and finding myself in deep water; constantly in the act of self-discovery. On-stage Len had nothing to do with off-stage Len, the confused man-boy who lost things travelling, drank too much, fell in love. But on-stage Len had to grasp a very adult craft, the art of which often eluded me.

Both the on-stage and off-stage Lens were a mess . . .

As a mimic, you're already putting on a mask. Nobody gets the chance to find out who you actually are. It's all pretend. Show business nowadays is all about bearing one's soul on stage, but back in the day, audiences didn't care who you were; they just wanted you to make them laugh, to walk on, wow them and walk off.

Older comedians would tell me that no one was interested in politics or your private life. If you did talk about your family, you always lied about what they were actually like; you created a different version of them. You *never* told the truth on stage; it was always a heightened world of pretence, where nothing was real. Irish people were thick, and black people were lascivious; housewives were randy, and salespeople even more so; all the policemen said, ''Ello, 'ello, 'ello, what's goin' on 'ere then?' This was a seaside postcard world where hangovers, big-chested blondes and giant sticks of rock were funny. People didn't reveal how unhappy they were; they just practised all those tropes that we'd come to expect in 1970s clubland. As I travelled the motorways of Great Britain in pursuit of my craft,

I found myself learning what was soon to become an outmoded comedy vocabulary.

For all immigrants, refugees and diaspora people, acquiring the language of your new home is a key tool of assimilation. If you're moving to a country where everybody speaks differently to you, being able to communicate is imperative. Fortunately, in the former British colonies English was the lingua franca, so we were one step ahead. But the way we spoke English, our Jamaican patois, was deemed unacceptable to some.

I always think it's funny when a Jamaican is interviewed on the news and there are subtitles. It seems perfectly clear to me what is being said: 'Mi guh down the street and mi si de man wid de gun come running,' sounds just like, 'I was walking down the street and I saw the assailant with the firearm approaching.' But to Middle England it sounds like gobbledegook, so people find ways to fix it. But not my brother Seymour, who, rather bravely and stubbornly, decided that he would always speak with a Yardie-style drawl, only speaking a super-stylised mockney, like a Jamaican Dick Van Dyke, when it suited him. Generally, this is a survival technique. By becoming one with your host country, you're sending out a message, which, to paraphrase, goes something like:

'There are universal things that bind us, and can't we all just get along? Look, I eat the same food as you, watch the same TV, listen to the same music. I even talk like you. I don't want any trouble. Please like me.'

That doesn't always work out, but for a lot of us it did. It doesn't mean bigotry and racism disappear as obstacles. Some people can't help showing their true colours under pressure. But for those who want to be ignored so that they can live their life in peace in this country, the idea of smoothing out the things that make you different is often adopted as the way to go.

Mimicry was a pathway; it was integration writ large. People do impressions because it marks them out, and they become *that* interesting person. It's a get-out-of-jail-free card for anybody who thinks they're a bit dull in real life. And similarly, if you can do a Glaswegian or Bristolian accent, you're the brown-skinned guy who 'talks like me'.

One of the things that's admired in the UK is being able to laugh at yourself. 'You don't want to have a chip on your shoulder, lad. You gotta be able to take a joke. If you can't, you'll never make it as a comic.' That becomes a currency too. But there's a danger: if you adopt the self-deprecating path, it has to be carefully negotiated so that you don't end up in a depressing spiral of self-perceived worthlessness. And I'm not sure anybody wants to watch that unless it's very skilfully handled, like Richard Pryor on racism, his difficult upbringing, his mother being a prostitute. Pryor's mimetic skills, writing prowess and prodigious talent enabled him to make jokes about any- and everything. Not everyone can do that.

Who Am I #12

This photograph was taken in Felixstowe in 1977. I was mid-summer season with John Hanson and the lovely Peter Butterworth. I'm in baggy flares and radio station t-shirt (I have no memory of Radio Orwell, though it probably wasn't *run by a Big Brother-type boss, with a room 101 where they'd send you if you cursed on air), while the guy with the floppy hair and squinting eyes is Roger Fotheringill; he used to sing and dance in the chorus of the show and we became buddies that summer.*

I look pretty happy – I'm fitting in – and everyone's smiling for the camera. It's all good. However, this relaxed feeling would soon vanish like steam off a hippo's backside during a heatwave, as 1978 and Great Yarmouth with the Black and White Minstrels Show *was just around the corner . . . sigh.*

7
Growing Up Fast

PAPA'S PASSING AND NINE NIGHTS

My relationship with my papa, Winston Jervis Henry (b.1918), was odd, to say the least. From the moment we met in 1959, I perceived a coldness between us. He never said, 'I love you,' or even, 'I like you.' He was distant towards me; he never gave a hug and kept his counsel. At mealtimes, apart from 'Stop the noise', he hardly said anything.

Papa was brilliant at growing things. One year he began marking out areas in our patchy backyard at Douglas Road, which was all dirt and scrabbly gravel. He planted some seeds and left them, hardly watering anywhere at all. When spring came, suddenly there were cabbages and potatoes and carrots and onions and courgettes. It was amazing. We'd all forgotten that in Jamaica, he and Mama had been subsistence farmers, able to coax growth out of any type of land, anywhere. Mama would look out of the window: 'Chuh! Him just a show-off . . .' And Papa would stand in the middle of it all, looking pleased with himself. We had to give vegetables away that year.

Papa could be frightening to us kids, although Mama had forbidden him to lay a finger on us. Usually, the role of the Jamaican papa is to be the rod of correction, the ultimate threat, but Mama did all that. She was the disciplinarian, she was the one that beat us when we'd done something wrong. As I said earlier, Papa rarely lashed out or hit us, but he did hit me once. I was tormenting Sharon (the youngest), and she was crying and yelling. I felt this very sharp sting in my side and bent double – WHOOF! And when I looked at Papa he was reading the paper. He had lashed out so fast that I hadn't even seen him do it. It was like getting a surreptitious beat-down from the Flash.

Papa would sometimes loom out of the shadows. One summer Bean's Industries was on strike, so Papa was at home a lot. I was running in and out of the house, drinking from the cold tap and then disappearing to the park for long stretches of time. Once, after an entire day of this, I came home to have my tea. The lights were dimmed and I was making my way through the kitchen to the dining table, where my supper awaited me. As I reached the table, Papa appeared out of nowhere. Shocked, I hiccupped, and suddenly gallons of water burst forth from my mouth. It went on for a good ninety seconds. It was like someone had hooked me up to a spigot and turned it on full blast – whoooooosh! We're talking gallons of water, everywhere. Papa just looked at me and said something like, 'I hope yu don't think is me cleaning that up?'

I spoke to Seymour and Hylton years later and asked if they'd ever had any moments with Papa that could be called intimate or personal. They thought for while, and then told me that once Papa started talking cricket, you couldn't stop him. They also said that he liked to talk about the shape of a beer glass. Not really 'intimate or personal', but I now wish I'd been present at those conversations.

The last few days of Papa's life stretched out into this hinterland of strangeness. He was suffering from renal failure, as well as dementia. This was a very difficult time for us as a family because before he was admitted into hospital, there had been shouting between him and Mama. Past relationship struggles suddenly snapped into focus and caused strife once more. Then Papa collapsed and was rushed into hospital, but he didn't last long. I was very conflicted by this turn of events. Papa had never shown any real concern or love for me. Why was I so worried about him getting sick? He'd never said more than five words to me at any given time.

I went to see him in hospital, and the odd thing was, he wanted to talk. And for the last few days of his life he talked constantly about pretty much every aspect of his life: Jamaica, growing up there, working the land there, how he could make just about anything grow, including ganja, and how he would harvest and carry the contraband in several crocus bags all over the district, selling it in order to feed his family. As I sat and listened to him I wanted to scream, 'Why didn't you do this before? Why couldn't we speak like this when I was growing up?'

But it was too late – within a few weeks he was dead.

In the lead-up to the funeral everyone was upset. Certainly, all the Jamaican-born Henry siblings were utterly distraught. Every one of them was crying – Seymour, Bev, Kay, Hylton – but me, Sharon and Paul were clueless as to why everyone was so upset. Mama wept copiously. How were we to survive on one wage packet? I didn't cry during the entire time.

Before a funeral there is a ritual in Jamaican culture called Nine Nights. During this time, the bereaved must play host to the friends and family of the deceased for nine nights, supplying food, drink and space so that the guests can say their goodbyes properly, without feeling rushed. Papa's Nine Nights began, and none of us Dudley-born Henrys knew what the hell was going on. Suddenly Caribbean people from all over the Black Country just started to appear at the front door:

'God bless Winston.'

'I worked with your father.'

'I knew your husband.'

'He was a good man.'

'He owed me five pound and I want it back.'

'I'm with him.'

The house was packed with these people for nine nights, all

drinking, eating, singing hymns, wiggling their hips, crying, sobbing, wailing. It was a nightmare. When I asked my mama what was going on, who were these people, etc., she merely patted me on the shoulder and said, 'This is just tradition.'

As the main rooms were filled with tearful or drunk guests, us Henry siblings found ourselves in the previously forbidden front room. This was a huge honour for us because indelibly printed on our cerebral cortexes were the words '*Yu mus' never enter the front room!*' We didn't understand the big deal; the room was the best-appointed space in the house, decorated with exotic flock wallpaper, leather(-ish) sofas adorned with hand-crocheted antimacassars, and lots of small paintings of Jesus – at the Last Supper, on the cross displaying his wounds . . . There were several framed texts on the wall. The one that scared me to death was:

> *Christ is the head of our house,*
> *The unseen guest at every meal,*
> *The silent listener to every conversation.*

To me this meant that Jesus's invisible head was floating around our house, lurking in the shadows, earwigging every conversation, like a kind of celestial CIA.

The front room had a massive drinks cabinet emblazoned with Japanese figures – geishas, samurai warriors, royal maidens. The radiogram was in there too, and this meant that my sister Kay could dominate proceedings with her taste in music. There'd be a bit of Aretha Franklin gospel, then when she thought the adults weren't paying attention she'd bust out 'Funk Funk' by Cameo, 'Serpentine Fire' by Earth, Wind & Fire and 'Got to Give It Up' by Marvin Gaye. The front room would soon be full of young people dancing. Mama would appear at the door and glare at us – and suddenly the gospel album would be back on.

My father's death did not hit me for many years after he'd passed. The sacrifices he'd made, the struggle against racism when he arrived in this country and the sheer slog of bringing home the bacon for years on end in a place that had been cold and uncharitable must have taken their toll.

The funeral ceremony – once it came – was long and drawn out. We had the service in the church and then the trip to the graveyard, where all the siblings took turns to shovel in the dirt. Once it was over, we all retired to a church hall and ate Jamaican food till we were full and drank till we were all drunk, and then I went back to work – I had things to do.

Shortly after that, Elvis died. He had a huge impact on me. Kay and I had watched all his films. I wanted to be him. All that stuff about him being a redneck emerged later. I always thought he looked like a decent chap, wiggling his hips and curling his lip all the while. How could he be a racist when his favourite music was black gospel? When he died at the age of forty-two, I was really upset. While I was growing up, Elvis's pictures were on my wall: clad in prison garb but bustin' moves in *Jailhouse Rock*, looking crazy handsome in *King Creole*. We had his records stuffed into the radiogram's storage space. Most of them were coverless, they had been played so many times. We had singles – 'Teddy Bear', 'Jailhouse Rock', 'Heartbreak Hotel' – and albums, but they were mostly cheap, knock-off versions, like *I Got Lucky*, which had a big shamrock on the front. We also had the *GI Blues* original soundtrack and the *Christmas Album*. I was a stone cold Elvis fan growing up; I had all the moves and had learnt songs like 'Jailhouse Rock', 'Blue Suede Shoes' and 'Hound Dog' off by heart. Elvis was one of the main reasons I got into show business.

Papa didn't give a monkey's about Elvis. When I was ten, we were all excited because Elvis's *Comeback Special* was going to be shown on BBC2. All the kids gathered round the TV and oohed and aahed at the King, all super-skinny in leather, grinning that devilish grin, making the girls in the crowd all crazy. My papa came in from work and said, 'Turn over the TV – I want to watch the cricket,' and that was that. No matter how much we bawled and complained and secretly muttered our hidden wish that Papa would suddenly be splidged by a falling piano, as the leader of the household what he said went, and we had to change channels to the boring-ass cricket. I hated him at that moment.

At the time of the funeral, I didn't hate him, I just wished I'd loved him more. I didn't cry, but I'm crying now as I write this because my papa raised me and put food on the table and clothes on my back. I owe him my tears. I grew up wearing a mask that said, 'My papa doesn't love me, I don't care,' but I had no idea of what he went through to raise me the way he did. I have memories of him and Mama arguing regularly about me – especially when I was younger, but I had no idea why. They'd come to blows sometimes, and either Kay or I would jump across the room to separate them, putting ourselves at risk. It didn't matter what we did, within days, or even hours sometimes, they'd be back at each other's throats.

DANNY AND THE HUMAN ZOO

In 2015 I dramatised these family tensions in *Danny and the Human Zoo*. I was working with my co-writer Jon Canter on creating *Cradle to Rave*, a music-based stage show that used elements of my life to tell the story of my love for music, whether it be rock, pop, soul or Kate Bush. Then I heard that Nicola Schindler and Caroline Hollick from Red Productions (famous for TV hits such as *Scott & Bailey*, *Last Tango in Halifax* and *Happy Valley*) wanted to talk to me about developing a TV series about my early life and my explosive introduction to the world of show business via *New Faces*.

Talks went on for a while, and soon the project had grown into a rite-of-passage story about a young black musician in Dudley and his chaotic Caribbean family. This iteration ran for a couple of years and the character of Danny grew into this loveable avatar that told stories from my life, but through music rather than comedy.

Then two things happened.

Firstly, the head of drama at the BBC, who would be the broadcaster for the project, wasn't sure if it should be four one-hour episodes. Secondly, they weren't *quite* sure that telling my story through the lens of music was actually what they *really* wanted. I'd given them liver and bacon, and what they wanted was jerk chicken and rice.

I sent a copy of the scripts to my friend, the legendary Neil Gaiman (*Coraline, Neverwhere, Anansi Boys, American Gods*). His notes, as always, were on the money:

Len, love Danny, love the family, love the Dudley stuff, but why isn't he a comedy impressionist?

P.S. This feels like a ninety-minute movie, rather than four one hours.

Xx Neil. Love to family.

Damn him! He was right. The closer the new version got to the truth, the easier it was for me to write. I wasn't having to make up scenarios and characters; I could riff on people I knew and the experiences I'd had and know that they would have the ring of truth. Perhaps the decision to avoid telling my own story so directly was driven by fear. In many respects I'm quite a private person and, apart from the odd mention in jokes, I tend to keep my family out of the glare of publicity.

However, *Danny and the Human Zoo* required a little

189

more about my family, experiences, triumphs and failures than I had previously been prepared to write. The shift in focus from Danny the musician to Danny the impressionist/ stand-up comedian gave me a sense of freedom. I could talk about things I knew about, albeit in a slightly refracted way. But there were things that had to be handled carefully, as with this memoir. My siblings were concerned that our parents' story would be exposed to public scrutiny. They asked if that was what I wanted.

It was a tough time because I wanted to write something that, if not completely truthful, was at least *my* truth. But there was a feeling in the family that I should sidestep the elephant in the room and not talk about my origins at all. However, when the penultimate draft of the script was completed, I sent it off to Seymour, Hylton, Bev, Kay, Sharon and Paul for their perusal. The general consensus was that it was funny, heart-felt and moving, and that I should proceed. Kay, however, was disappointed and thought it didn't go far enough. She believed there was an element of pussyfooting around the truth with the fictionalisation of the family and the attempt to 'dress up' my origins in an accessible-to-Middle-England way. I re-assured her that I would do the best I could with the resources that we had.

In many ways, *Danny and the Human Zoo* is the precursor to this memoir. Once I had the taste of storytelling and life-mapping in my mouth, I had the feeling that there was more to say about being a young man growing up in the Black Country in the 1960s and early '70s. The film was the first time I had been able to communicate to the world at large about who I truly was and where I came from. Sometimes I wish I hadn't done so – the subsequent press attention was horrible and intrusive. My brothers and sisters were harangued by local and national reporters, all vying for a scoop about my secret origins. I don't know if I will ever quite recover from everyone knowing my business.

Now that I'm Big People myself, I've learnt that story ownership is the least of one's problems. Big People have to sort out kids and lovers and wives and husbands and work and career and bills and house maintenance and relationships with their neighbours and Brexit and sexism and racism and homophobia, and deal with the fact that *Coronation Street* is getting its first black family almost sixty years after the series began. Big People have to deal with a lot; sometimes it's good to let the kids run along and play and not worry about adult concerns.

Throughout every single family crisis, I grew like a weed, ate like a trencherman and played games of kick the can, hide-and-seek and wall-ball over in Buffery Park. There were beatings and chastisements, but there were also physical acts of love: hugs, pats on the head, laughter, smiles and mountains of food served up every day. There was no absence of love in our house; for the most part, it was unspoken, but we all felt safe within its walls. There was love; I just didn't know what it looked, felt or smelt like at the time . . .

Once the secret of my origin had been revealed, the next few years featured a great deal of guilt and shame on my part. I thought the entire world already knew this big secret, one that I was the last to discover. Whenever I was up in Dudley, the embarrassment of clocking one's birth father was palpable. Sometimes I'd see him when I was in the park with the Grazebrook Crew. They had no idea why I would suddenly clam up and try to shrink myself down as this black guy came towards me. Bertie had no fear of chatting to me whenever or wherever we met. He might amble out of some pub, see me across the street and yell at the top of his voice, 'LEN!' and I'd have to cross the road and say hello to him. He might give me some pocket money . . . *in front of people*. I would die. But I think he was only trying to make the best of a cataclysmically bad job.

Clearly, he wanted to bond, but to me it felt too late. In my early teens I overnighted a few times at his bedsit. It was strangely intimate – we had to sleep in the same bed. There was a huge chamber pot that we were both required to use during the night. Then in the morning he'd put *The Archers* on and make breakfast, as I tidied the room and set the table. I can't remember what we spoke about at these times. I was a mute visitor who chose to speak only when questioned directly. I imagine most questions were along the lines of 'How's your mother?'

The main feeling I had about the whole 'new dad' situation was that although Bertie was my father by blood, Winston – whether he liked it or not – was the guy who had raised me, put up with me, watched me grow through my early childhood. This new situation was interesting, but it didn't change the infrastructure. I grew into my teens knowing I had to factor in this other person. I tried to avoid him as best I could, but he was a constant presence. I wanted to say, 'Why are you here *now*? Where were you *before*?' but I wasn't brave enough.

BECOMING ADULT

After Papa's funeral I went back to London, back to work, leaving my Dudley cares and woes behind.

I was gaining experience, though: twenty-seven episodes of *The Fosters*; I'd worked with Arthur Mullard and Irene Handl; I was spending time with Norman Beaton and the rest of the *Fosters* cast; I was hanging out with the Lockshen Gang and learning what it was to be 'London'. My accent was adapting into a kind of mockney whenever I was there. Mind you, because I was a mimic, wherever I went I seemed to take on the accent of that place. My survival technique on the road was to blend in, fit in, h'integrate!

And it seemed to work: wherever I went, the locals thought I was from there, and that suited me. I would do anything to knock down a barrier, just to make my progress easier. It was hard enough just showing up somewhere and doing a show for one night or three days or a week; I didn't need people picking on me because I was from the Black Country and talked funny. I wanted them to like me. Comedians are generally quite needy people. I was no different.

And that's how I went into 1978. Papa was no longer around, and I was the family's main breadwinner. I loved being able to help my sibs out financially with a new carpet, couch or school uniform. Although I was one of the youngest, show business had conferred adulthood on me. I was ambivalent about this: on the one hand, it was good to have the facility to be generous, but at times the responsibility was a burden.

The Fosters had gone, as LWT didn't want it any more. But there were further commitments with the Black and White Minstrels. There was a winter season in Coventry that year. I was dreading it but had to pick up the gauntlet and get on with it. After all, this is what I had chosen to do. Four years of being in show business and I was still entrenched in the bowels of minstrelsy, but my brain was beginning to change gears. How could I get out of this? The show kept on rolling, like a huge tank grinding and crunching its way into enemy territory.

Relationships at the time were fun but short. All I remembered from growing up was people shouting at each other, stuck in a relationship that had perhaps run its course. Marriage seemed to be a snare that our parents were continually trying to escape, gnawing their feet off at the ankle – anything to get away. When I went to my white friends' houses, I saw compromise. People tended to keep their relationship chatter tightly bound and locked away in their bedrooms, whereas in Jamaican families – and mine in particular – everybody's business just seemed to detonate and wipe out anybody within a 200-yard radius. Jamaicans are passionate, emotional and unafraid of facing up to whatever issues are troubling them. It all spills out, whether they want it to or not.

I'm pretty sure that this – at times hostile – home environment often frightened me into being emotionally inert. I wanted the tactile side of things, but when it came to the deeper connective tissues of romantic love, I would freeze and start looking for a way out. The further I was able to get away from the influence of my parents, the more I learnt that you could be stable, faithful and true in a relationship. But in some ways this was wishful thinking. A lot of the time I'd drift into a relationship, then drift out, without even realising it.

The work was the thing back then. I didn't have any big plans, except for a nagging feeling that my life would be so much better if only I could get out of *The Black and White Minstrel Show*.

Who Am I #13

This shot of me from 1978 is an example of how deeply immersed in mid-1970s light entertainment I was. Any other twenty-year-old black guy in this period could be seen in Oxford bags, tennis shoes, leather jacket, beret or leather tam, dark glasses, exotic cigarette the size of a small rolled-up carpet, clenched fist, etc. Here's me, neatly cut hair, toothy smile, beige tuxedo, massive velvet bow tie, grinning as if to say to all the world, 'Hey, Middle England, don't worry, I'm as safe as safe can be!' And I was! I just wanted to learn how to do my job and get better at it. I didn't want to smash the oppressor or kill Whitey. I wanted to smash box-office records and buy my mama a house.

DAVID LUTON

David Luton was Mike Hollis's driver and record-box car-
rier. They were as thick as thieves, and I was envious of their
effortless cool. Davey was from up Oakham way and still lived
with his mum, although he acted as if he didn't. I knew something was going on when he came to see me during the 1978
summer season. I was with the Minstrels at the Britannia Pier
in Great Yarmouth, and he'd called up to ask if he could crash
at mine. He was recovering from a doomed relationship with
a nurse and needed somewhere to chill. I told him he could
come and stay with me. He drove over, and it was great – here
was someone I knew who was willing to help me endure my
prison sentence with the Minstrels and party with me afterwards, helping me to forget what I was doing between 6.10
and 10.40 p.m. every night.

One time Davey came into the theatre with me, helping me
carry freshly pressed shirts and hanging them up. We laughed
a little as show time approached, and then he disappeared to
give me some 'me' time before I hit the stage. I went on and did
my twelve minutes, and when I came off stage and reached my
dressing room, I opened the door to find my normally chaotic
and messy dressing room completely tidied and squared away.
Davey had done everything possible to make my working environment pristine.

I told him I was impressed and thankful. I also told him that
what he had done was very important. I asked him if he wanted
a full-time job helping me do what I had to do. He said yes,
and after that he was by my side for every show, driving me to
each venue, organising the dressing room, finding someone to
press suits and shirts, making sure we had four-way sockets, a
table, a chair. Davey sorted out the backstage rider: were there

sandwiches, soft drinks, herbal and builders' tea? Shoes polished? On-stage water, table and stool prepared? Props sorted? Throat sweets? He did everything it was possible to do backstage to make the on-stage aspect run smoothly.

Davey had a habit of speaking his mind when perhaps holding one's counsel might have been the preferred route. We had arguments sometimes, always about hierarchy. Davey didn't like being told what to do, but unfortunately neither of us was telepathic; someone had to take responsibility for getting us to the venue, into the dressing room, onto the stage. Sometimes the rows were about finding our way to the venue, the inadequacy of dressing rooms, forgetting shirts or socks, losing vocal warm-up tapes. But I always forgave him.

Davey was a godsend. He made each day bearable and liveable when I was on the road. There were some days when I was completely and utterly depressed by the whole thing and just wanted to disappear. Like when a renowned club owner wanted to pay me in cash or not at all, or when another owner stormed backstage because one of the dancers had torn her leg open against one of my props. No matter what I said, the manager wouldn't back down and calm himself. But Davey managed to talk everyone down off the roof. He was good like that. He saw me at my best and my worst; he endured bad tempers, stupid behaviour, shouting, the works, and hardly ever complained. However, he always stuck up for himself, fought the good fight and never backed down. Sometimes this was hard for me to deal with, but we got through, and Davey had my back in both good times and bad.

He was deeply loyal. He stayed quiet when we were at work, doing his tasks and ticking them off one by one with quiet satisfaction. He'd join in with the banter and wisecracks when he thought it was appropriate, but he was always there to help me. That's his voice you can hear at the beginning of my stand-up shows, like *Live and Unleashed* and *Lenny Go Home*. I wanted a Dudley accent on the mic introducing the show, and boy did we get it:

LAYDEEZ 'N' GENNELMEN, GIVE IT UP FOR LENNAY HENRAAAAAAY!

Thanks, chap. You were bostin'.

GROWTH SPURT, 1978

The Minstrels invaded Great Yarmouth. I'd never been there before and didn't know what to expect. The show was going to be shaken up this time as there was no Don Maclean – he had gone his own way. The line-up was the ventriloquist Keith Harris, with Orville the duck and Cuddles the monkey; Sheffield-born comic Bobby Knutt, with whom I shared a dressing room; and me doing my usual second-spot comedy slot. By now I'd done roughly the same set for four years on the trot. I had fallen down a rabbit hole of complacency, laziness and fulfilling the audience's expectations. You want a stupid, self-deprecating joke about blackness?

(wiping sweat from my brow) *'I'm leaking . . .'*
(tasting it) *'It's chocolate!'*

I had loads of those, but I tried to keep them to a minimum. I couldn't steal all of Charlie Williams's act – my tenure as Don Maclean's one-night-only replacement in Blackpool had taught me that. I needed new material, and fast.

Don had put me in touch with a writer he knew called Howard Imber, who lived in Grantham and churned out one-liners for Don, me and various others. Howard didn't try to impose a personality on me or a point of view; he just wrote jokes and I would tick the ones I liked. It was a methodology I would employ until I met Kim Fuller in 1980 on *Three of a Kind*.

Keith Harris was in his pomp in 1978. He was a reliable act. He'd start with Cuddles the monkey, who was genuinely funny. Mums, dads and kids would wet themselves as Cuddles heckled, interfered and got in the way of whatever Keith was trying to do:

Keith: 'And now, ladies and gentlemen . . .'
Cuddles: 'I want to go wee.'
Keith: 'What? Not now, I'm busy. Ladies and g—'
Cuddles: 'I want to go wee – now.'
Keith: 'You can't. Sorry about this, ladies and gentlemen . . . what do you mean?'
Cuddles: 'It's coming out . . .'
Keith: 'What? Don't . . . Ladies and gentlemen, if you could just –'
Cuddles: 'I. WANT. TO. GO. WEE.'
Keith: 'Oh, go on then.'
Cuddles: 'WEEEEEEEEEEEEEEEEEEEE!'

I never understood why Keith opened with Cuddles and finished with Orville, the duck that couldn't fly. It was cloying and got 'aahhhs' rather than big laughs. Still, that was his business, not mine. Keith was a proper leader when it came down to it. He saw that my props were less than below standard and helped me make some new ones – Trevor McDonald glasses and moustache combined, a Miss Piggy nose, etc. – without asking for payment; he just wanted me to represent myself on stage in the best way I could. I was gobsmacked by this act of kindness, totally floored.

Although Keith would close part one of the show with Cuddles, part two of the show was different. Keith would walk on, crack a few gags. I would walk on from the side and we would perform 'Old MacDonald Had a Farm'. Every time

Keith touched my back, I would open and close my mouth – instant ventriloquist's dummy! Keith had done this before with other people, but I genuinely believed him when he said this was the best the routine had gone.

On stage with Keith I was freed from the tyranny of my act. I was proving to myself that given the material, I could get laughs doing whatever I wanted. This routine, although simple, allowed me to work off someone else and to ad-lib. I had already found that when things went wrong on stage, the audience noticed immediately and wanted the act to comment on or improvise around the situation. Keith and I were good at messing around when this happened. In one show I sneezed during the number and my nose immediately gushed blood everywhere. Keith likened the whole thing to a Sam Peckinpah movie, while I did the slow-motion spurting. It was funny for a while, but then I had to get off the stage because blood was going all over my suit.

Sharing a dressing room with Bobby Knutt was interesting. He had been in a Ken Loach film called *The Price of Coal*, a ground-breaking BBC1 *Play for Today* about northern miners who were about to go on strike and its effect on their families. Knutty had given a wonderful performance. He was also a successful comic who had honed his craft in some of the most brutal clubs in the UK. Knutty was fearless and he gave me a kick up the arse. He saw every show as an opportunity to tweak material, to try something new, to fiddle with everything. He never complained about being in the Minstrels' show; he just did his routine and then went back to his dressing room. I took to watching him every time he performed and got a sense of what was going on when he was on the mic. He had poise and a storyteller's calm.

Once the season began, it trundled and rumbled and rolled on. Larry Grayson was up the road doing a show, Little and Large were nearby and the legendary Frank Carson was also there with a *Comedians*-type stage show. There was a bar called The Gordon's, where we'd all meet afterwards. Lots of territory-marking took place as the professional comedians took it in turns to crack gags about each other, a kind of comedy roast as you went to get your drink: 'Alright, lad. I heard they had t'undertaker waiting for you the other night after you'd done your act.' Generally, though, people were kind. You had the odd person who might throw in the occasional racist comment, but I tended to turn a blind eye to that. Besides, there was too much going on. Yarmouth had loads of nightclubs, discos and bars, enough nightlife to stifle even the liveliest of nihilistic urges!

Music would be a prime catalyst for me over the next few years. It was the thing that got me up in the morning, put me in the mood for the show, made my soul soar in the evenings after I'd finished. Music kept me on the straight and narrow and also pushed depression away. I was functioning and not allowing myself to be swallowed by despair.

Who Am I #14

This is me, Keith Harris and Eddie Large. I loved working with Keith; in fact, I loved working with anybody! Misery loves company . . . In this period I'm grabbing at the coat-tails of anyone who might lead me where I want to go. Keith,

*with his bubble perm, very tight trousers and slick patter,
was the perfect guy for a nineteen-year-old to hang out with.
He knew all the clubs, DJs and bartenders. It was like being
a junior member of the Rat Pack. I don't remember paying
for anything. What I do remember is lots of drunken nights,
laughing hysterically as Keith made various inanimate objects
talk in different voices with different accents.*

*We'd do dance routines. We'd go to clubs and they'd play
'One Nation Under a Groove', and Keith and I would bust
out a little routine that we'd practised. It involved quick flicks,
turns, hand-raises and a high five. I know it sounds weird, but
at the time it felt important that we could get down in sync like
this. There was a certain amount of hero-worshipping going
on here. I even went on holiday with Keith to Corfu. This was
in 1978. I'd never been abroad before, so I took all my stage
suits, props and a sheepskin coat with me. I spent the entire two
weeks in Speedos, sandals and a T-shirt. Crazy days. I learnt a
lot from him. And this is me in the midst of it all.*

I think I was spoilt by my first pantomime appearance, working in *Aladdin* at Bournemouth Pavilion. This period of my life seems to have blurred, as if a small, inquisitive child has plastered sticky paint over a living-room wall, so I can't remember the exact date; let's just say it was late 1970s. I was the Genie of the Lamp. The difficulty of this was figuring out how I could do what the audience wanted to see. How could the genie do impressions like Lenny would? The producer, Maurice Fournier, said, 'It's simple: although he's been stuck in the lamp for centuries, what he's been doing recently is watching 1970s television,' which gave me permission to momentarily escape the 2D confines of the fake lamp and do a six-minute bit in the first half; then rinse and repeat in the second half.

It was a hugely enjoyable experience. A number of the people who had been in the Minstrels were also in the chorus line of *Aladdin*. But there was no blacking-up for the male dancers, no jokes about 'Lenny not having to wear make-up too'. I enjoyed pantomime a lot, even though I quickly surmised that kids could smell my fear from several miles away. I had no clue how to entertain children; my act was aimed squarely at an adult audience. So I stuck to the things I'd done on television, but often the kids wanted more.

When I worked in *Jack and the Beanstalk* at Lewisham Town Hall, I did a routine with Keith Harris set in a custard-pie factory. The conveyor belt speeded up as we worked, so eventually we wound up with shaving foam in every crevice of our bodies. The very young audience loved the whole taboo of adults behaving like children on stage. However, I never really saw myself as a children's entertainer. Even at the age of fifteen I wanted to make Big People laugh.

ENTER CHRIS TARRANT

In the meantime, unbeknownst to me Frank Carson had encouraged Chris Tarrant, the producer and lead presenter of the rambunctious Saturday-morning kids' show *Tiswas*, to come and see me in the Minstrels' show. I had a feeling that the Black and White Minstrels would most definitely *not* be Tarrant's bag, but I was glad he was coming and just hoped he'd be impressed by my bits. Then, disaster!

Keith Harris had bronchitis and no voice, which meant that Orville and Cuddles couldn't talk either! So Keith was out of the show, and I was designated to be compère for the night. Fortunately, I now had enough material to link the show together on my own, without using anyone else's jokes. Tarrant was in the house, so I wanted to do my best. *Tiswas* had been running since 1974 and was gaining a reputation for anarchy and reckless behaviour, live and direct on your TV set every Saturday morning. Frank had recommended me for the show, and I didn't want to let him down.

The night of the show, *sans* Keith. I am the host and, in a hastily rehearsed sequence, I'm escorted down some shiny stairs by the beautiful, sky-high, sequinned and befeathered Television Toppers. As I get to the stage, I slip and split my trousers. I get up *immediately* and attempt to regain my dignity by doing some impromptu crowd work, messing around with the front row, and eventually leave the stage with my hands covering the offending rip in my pants. I think I can see a blond hulk wetting himself in the audience.

I come back and do the rest of my pieces, and then the show is over. Afterwards Tarrant doesn't even come backstage to say hello. I'm thinking, 'Useless. He didn't like it.'

I spend most of the next week moaning about this to Frank

Carson whenever I see him. I call Tarrant as many names under the sun as I can conjure from the furthest reaches of my nasty mind. None of them do justice to the way I'm feeling. Then, one fateful evening, as I arrive at the stage door of the Britannia Pier, Great Yarmouth, the stage doorman gives me an envelope. It contains a handwritten letter from Chris Tarrant:

Dear Len
  Would you like to pop down to ATV studios when Tiswas *is back on the air and have a look at what we're doing down there?*
  All the best, C.T.

And a drawing of a fish.

Great news! It certainly gave me the energy and the impetus to plough through to the end of the summer season. I'd also begun discussions with BBC Midlands and Don Maclean about a sketch show called *The Cheapest Show on the Telly*, so things were looking good. It would be screened only in the Midlands, mind, but at least I had work.

Don lived in the posh part of Brum, a place called Solihull. We would meet at his house to discuss what we might do in the show. I wasn't sure about the title – didn't that sound like we were doing rubbish telly? Don was adamant that there would be no fancy sets or costumes. It would be very much a no-frills-type show: very few costumes, even fewer sets. TV at its most basic.

There'd be an opening double-act bit that Don and I would do, then lots of sketches. Don had a working relationship with a guy called Gid Taylor, who was a folkie songwriter who helped us with parodies of all kinds. I did a parody of John Travolta's solo number 'Sandy' from *Grease*:

> *Stranded in the car park*
> *Feelin' such a berk*

What will they say
Monday at work . . .

We did two series of *The Cheapest Show on the Telly*, and my favourite part of it all was the time spent with my mentor Don. He really pushed me on every episode, helped me to think about the material we were being given. We also worked together on a BBC1 Saturday-night summer variety show called *Seaside Special*, and it was a hoot. But I was wary of people thinking that we were a double act. I knew that in my heart of hearts I was a single act. However rubbish I was at this stage ('great for 5 minutes but becomes unspooled after 25' – *Dudley Herald*), I valued the freedom of working on my own.

But whatever my innermost feelings about *The Cheapest Show*, it was a stepping stone to the next stage of my life. I jumped.

8

Tiswas

TODAY IS SATURDAY – WATCH AND SUFFER!

I responded to Chris Tarrant's invitation to go down and watch an episode of *Tiswas* go out live. It was a chaotic mess, and I loved it. He hired me, which would lead to a massive, unforeseen change in my career.

I started work on the show at the end of 1978. I was as rough as a wolverine's scabby arse, standing there trying to repeat my *New Faces* success in a format that was less traditional, less cabaret, less organised than mainstream telly. I was learning, whenever Tarrant could bear to have me on again, that a chaotic, anarchic Saturday-morning show was not the place to get up and do a short structured set. They wanted more than that. They wanted you to contribute throughout, not just perform one spot and disappear.

So that was me on *Tiswas*, thinking I was doing OK, but then watching John Gorman playing wild and anarchic characters such as Smello (who would release stink bombs when making an entrance), the irretrievably Scouse Masked Poet and PC Plod the thick copper, dropping in, getting a laugh and disappearing, then popping up again as a different character.

Tarrant would tell me off when he thought I hadn't been funny, which was often. I would get really upset, but he always made it up to me by taking me out for lunch the day before the show. He would plough through an enormous plate of moules marinière, accompanied by a bottle of good red wine, and go through the previous week's show with me, telling me what worked and what didn't. I would listen to him week after week. This was valuable feedback.

I loved watching Chris and his co-presenter Sally James at the desk. They made live television look so easy. Kids would be everywhere, and Chris would leave the desk and run across the studio floor to pick up a bucket of ice-cold water and hurl it at some students trapped in a cage; then he'd reach up and pull on a lever, and they'd be well and truly gunged by a mixture of shaving foam, water and vegetable dye. He'd then run back to the desk and resume his position, saying, 'Well, there you are! Marvellous!' Or, 'This is the stuff, this is what they want. Never mind the *Multi-Coloured Swap Shop* with Noel Edmonds, that smoothie with his popinjay beard and simpering voice. We don't want that, we want *this*!' – and he'd get up and throw more buckets of water at the trapped innocents.

I spent more time laughing on *Tiswas* than on any other show. The rest of them had been on the programme since 1974, so by 1978 there was a real sense that the juggernaut was on the road and pretty much unstoppable. The viewing figures were very good by comparison to our direct competition, the BBC's *Multi-Coloured Swap Shop*. But the devil was in the detail. *Tiswas*'s audience was different to Noel Edmonds's: we were told that 51 per cent of our audience was over eighteen. The people that wrote to the show asking to be in the cage weren't little kids, they were firefighters and doctors and nurses and students and teachers and mechanics and Sunday-football players. Hell's Angels would write asking for one of Sally's garter belts.

Tarrant attracted folk club-type comics like Max Boyce and Jasper Carrott. They came on the show and got bucketed good and proper, but also became honorary team members. Tarrant and John Gorman were invited to appear at the closing ceremony of an Eisteddfod in Cardiff, where they appeared on the same bill as Boyce and a Welsh male voice choir. As the choir began to sing 'Land of My Fathers', there was uproar as the Phantom Flan Flinger invaded proceedings and, with the help of Flanderella and the Baby Bucket Bunger, began to systematically take the choir apart with foamy custard pies and buckets of water. Boyce, plastered in gunge, just kept repeating, 'Never in the annals of history have we seen anything like this, boyo. Never . . .'

Jasper Carrott bestowed the Dying Fly on the show. This was a routine whereby members of the *Tiswas* fan club would lie on their backs and kick their arms and legs in time to the music. Kids were getting into trouble by doing this routine near railway lines and on dual carriageways. We eventually stopped this madness as people were getting upset with us.

After the first two series, something released in me. Tarrant's guidance had begun to sink in, and I started to think properly about what I could do every week on the show. Everyone on the production team seemed to want me to succeed, but no one tried to push me into doing something I didn't want to do, and I really appreciated that.

It would take me at least another eighteen months to really find my feet. Fairly early on we had discovered that my idiosyncratic impression of the ITN reporter Trevor McDonald (or McDonut, as we called him) was really handy. I could pop up anywhere and do a series of newsflashes (written by Graham Deykin, Howard Imber or David McKellar), which would get a laugh, and then I'd be drenched with ice-cold water. Tarrant would throw the buckets himself and took great pleasure in hurling them as aggressively as he could.

There was a whole subculture around the *Tiswas* posse. They were party people, so when the show ended at 12.30 p.m., we'd all go to the bar for a post-mortem, which usually ended up with all of us (apart from Sal) getting very drunk and laughing a lot. There was a lot of pitching for the next week's show. I remember comedian Norman Collier (a fellow *Tiswas* aficionado) crawling on his hands and knees, trying to explain that he was a deep-sea diver who couldn't follow a map. It never got on the show, but we laughed our heads off in the bar while he was improvising it. Tarrant loved Frank Carson's bizarre turns on the show. The recurring idea was that Frank was always trying to get on the show to promote whatever he was doing at the time. He'd come on in disguise and pretend to be a reporter or a Mystic Meg-type character, and Tarrant, mid-routine, would always sniff out his true identity: 'Hang on, I recognise that reddened bulbous nose, those rotting stump teeth! That ridiculous accent! You're not a respected reporter. I put it to you that you are Frank Carson! Get out!!' Sometimes he'd start hitting Frank and calling him names. It was nearly always a major-league hoot. Later, they'd go to a really rough pub called The Gary Owen, which served food and drinks way, way into the night, and crack gags and laugh for hours. I only ever did that once or twice – those guys could really drink. I was a lightweight and couldn't keep up.

But the momentum of the show was unstoppable. It seemed that whatever happened on the show on a Saturday morning became 'water cooler' chat the following Monday morning. One week Sally James is being sawn in half by a magician. John Gorman mutters, 'I bet I get the half that eats,' and the whole studio collapses with laughter. Bernard Manning steps on a 'speak your weight' machine, and the thing explodes, bleating in a robotic, Dalek-style voice, 'One. At. A. Time. Please!' Phil Collins from Genesis stands in a plant pot, as I, dressed as David Bellamy, talk about 'Gwoing pwog wock plants using vawious types of manure to encouwage gwowth.'

Loads of people made guest appearances: Michael Palin and Terry Jones, Jim Davidson, Status Quo, Annie Lennox, Paul McCartney and Wings, Motörhead, Billy Idol, the Pretenders . . . There was something of the zeitgeist about the show. We didn't really understand why it had become this televisual force

218

to be reckoned with, but clearly it demanded our full attention and hard work. So we pushed ourselves. Tarrant certainly felt that there was more potential to this live anarchy lark than he had at first thought. As my confidence grew and I met other writers and creators, I started to suggest people who could work on the show. More than thirty shows a year was a lot when you considered that Chris was responsible for each one. He relied on us to come up with our own bits and pieces to sprinkle throughout. So we did.

Although Tarrant was a bit of a tyrant, I think the process used in creating the show, with us chipping in, was what made it so successful. Everyone had ideas, which we were encouraged to pitch every week. There wasn't a set format, apart from a very rough template that Chris worked from:

Pre-titles
Titles
Today's menu
Smello interrupts
Menu continues
Frank Spencer in balcony interrupt
Sally James link to:
Pop video
First commercial break

It would continue like that for two and a half hours.

Chris produced this show, with the help of a diligent and hard-working team, from 1974 through till 1982. Later, in the 1990s, Channel 4's *The Big Breakfast* would churn out five shows a week on a year-round basis (as one of its hosts, Johnny Vaughan, pointed out to me, 'You guys had it easy'), but at the time we felt like we were the hardest-working team in television.

There was still the ever-present vibe of dissatisfaction. What the hell was I *still* doing in *The Black and White Minstrel Show*? Nobody talked about it at the *Tiswas* offices, but I could tell they pitied me. *Tiswas* was brilliant, as far as I was concerned; it was a release for me and I threw myself into it wholeheartedly. My favourite times on the show are the ones you'd imagine, such as when a tiny child called Matthew Butler wore a rabbit suit and sang 'Bright Eyes' from *Watership Down*. The first time I saw this little boy trying to sing in tune and failing, I laughed so hard my eyeballs nearly fell out. I also loved it when the entire team dressed as rabbits to sing along and dance to Chas and Dave performing their hit 'Rabbit'.

When I was working in panto up north at the Civic Hall in Middleton, Chris and John Gorman showed up to support their fellow *Tiswas* colleague. It was great to have them in the audience cheering me on as I was doing *Tiswas*-related material. I did an Algernon Winston Churchill (etc.) Razamatazz routine with the pantomime cow. At just the right moment, I accidentally on purpose threw a tiny amount of water onto the front row, splattering Tarrant and Gorman as they sat there. I saw Tarrant's eyebrows arch upwards – this was WAR! He disappeared.

My routine continued, but then suddenly I couldn't see anything because I was drenched. The musicians were running away because the organ, drums and electrical equipment had begun fizzing. Thanks to Tarrant, it was all completely sodden, a major fire hazard.

I ran off and grabbed another bucket. Soon more of the front row were soaked. Gorman went off somewhere, and next minute he was *on stage*, upending a bucket on my head.

The audience were delighted that the two hairy-arsed blokes from *Tiswas* were creating havoc. What had been quite a conventional afternoon of genteel pantomime fun had become complete and utter ANARCHY! Needless to say, I was the one that got well and truly bollocked. I was determined to get my revenge, but Tarrant and Gorman had snuck out before the finale.

Even though I wasn't particularly experienced at pantomime, I did learn new skills every time I performed. The audience, full of under-tens, may still have filled me with dread, but at least I had some experience of how to cope with that. My advice – RUN!

Who Am I #15

*This is a press pic of me looking bright-eyed, bushy-tailed and
ready for action. I'm nineteen and I've got a sort of Afro that's
growing upwards rather than outwards, but I'm also relaxed
and smiling – and it seems like a real smile. What's interesting is
the unstructured, ungroomed air about the picture. If you were
designing this shot for some campaign, you might have pressed
the shirt and jeans and combed, or at least trimmed, my hair. I
look like I'm ready to take on the entire universe . . . but I get
a sense that at the time I wasn't aware of the cannonball that
was coming my way. (Getty)*

THE REAL TREVOR MCDONUT

A huge, seminal moment for me on *Tiswas* was when Trevor McDonald interrupted one of my comedy bits as a big surprise. I was mid-joke:

Owing to severe cutbacks at the BBC the children's programmes Crackerjack, Wacky Races *and* Jackanory *are to be amalgamated. The new show is to be called* Crackerwackyjackernackernory.

I'm almost at the punchline when I feel a tap on my shoulder. Tarrant's shaggy visage is an inch away from my face, and he's grinning, full of mischief. I look just past him and see Trevor Mc-Feckin'-Donald smiling at me. He improvs some banter, along the lines of 'You've taken my job,' and 'Move over and let the real thing have a go.' It takes me a second to get my bearings. When I see him properly, I start saying, 'Hello, Daddy. And how is Mummy coming along?' – the first thing that enters my mind, obviously. I'm in the presence of a legend, and I'm talking utter bollocks. He sits in my place, and I roar with laughter when I read on the monitor the caption that appears beneath his image: 'The Real Trevor McDonut'.

Trevor has made further appearances on shows I've been involved with. He always says yes and has become a good friend and colleague in subsequent years.

THE *TISWAS* EPIPHANY

My big epiphany regarding *Tiswas* came during my second Blackpool season in 1980, this time with Cannon and Ball. I was freaking because I knew the new series of *Tiswas* was coming up in the autumn, and my brain was wrecked. What new material did I have for the series? I had literally nothin', zilch, zip, *nichts*. Luckily, I'd been hanging out with David McKellar, Cannon and Ball's writer on their LWT show. McKellar was Oxbridge, lived in Brighton and was a Monty Python fan. He had shoulder-length hair, wore sunglasses all the time and, more importantly, was incredibly enthusiastic. He enjoyed working with Tommy and Bob, but he could also sniff out a main chance when it was looking him in the eye. He saw that I was seeking to make a change to my set-up at *Tiswas* and offered to help. He identified that the 'churn' aspect of the programme was a killer for a comic like me. What I needed were repeatable characters who did the same thing every week – just with different material.

I wanted to play a Rastafarian character called Algernon Winston Spencer Churchill Gladstone Disraeli Pitt the Elder, the Younger. There was a record out by a singer named Errol Dunkley called 'OK Fred', so Algernon's catchphrase was: 'Oooooooooooooookaaaaaaaaaaaaaaaaaaaaaaaaaaaaaaaaaaaaa-aaaaaaaaaaaaaay!' The longer you could make it last, the better. Days after the character debuted on the programme, kids began approaching me in the street and challenging me to an 'Okay-off'. They'd stand there, with their parents waiting patiently, and look up at me, squeaking out an 'Okay' for as long as they could, till they were blue in the face.

Algernon also ate condensed-milk sandwiches, like my papa. Winston's recipe of buttered hard-dough bread with as much condensed milk as you fancied in the middle went down a storm, and soon children from diverse backgrounds all over the country were trying B&C sandwiches. Algernon was a hit. Having McKellar on board meant that now there were specially written recurring vehicles, such as 'Rural Retreats', where Chris and I, as David Bellamy, would go out and about and act the goat. We pre-filmed in the sea at Blackpool and in the amusement park; I played Trevor McDonut rising from the waves. Suddenly I was being given more to do. McKellar wrote a long-form sketch called 'Pulsebeat' for Trevor, and there were quiz-type formats where Trevor had so many rules to get through that by the time he got to the end of them, the programme was over. We did the Reverend Nathaniel Westminster ('but you can call me Nat West'), the Samurai double act and many other things, all interspersed with buckets of water and custard pies . . . rinse and repeat.

The studio floor was a health-and safety-nightmare: you could cut yourself on the sharp edge of a desk or the cage, you could slip on soapy water, you could accidentally inhale shaving foam (happened to me twice), which would leave you gasping for air. You could have passed out, but everyone would just laugh and throw more water at you. Utter chaos.

Who Am I #16

This is an early Tiswas *gang shot. At the front is John Gorman as PC Plod, wearing a loose tie and police uniform (strangely laid-back). Sally James and Chris Tarrant take centre spot. I'm on the left at the back (as if you couldn't guess), with my mouth*

as wide as I can get it, à la Animal in The Muppet Show. *Next to me is future Doctor Who Sylvester McCoy, ATV continuity announcer Peter Tomlinson, and then the legend in his own mind, Frank 'That's a cracker/It's the way I tell 'em' Carson.*

This is very similar to almost every picture taken of me during this period. I'm either laughing or shrieking with a kind of unalloyed pleasure; there are children around (mostly white) and Tarrant is mid-broadcast. The common theme is chaos, laughter and naughtiness – Tiswas *was all about transgressing the boundaries of what was generally allowed on a Saturday-morning kids' show.*

My journeys to Birmingham from 1978 to 1981 always seemed to involve a momentary dropping of whatever mask I was wearing at the time. The process of generating the chaos that was Tiswas *involved a bit of work, to say the least, but it was fun. And I was desperate to stay in it and be one of the gang.*

Not only was it fun, but everybody seemed to watch it! There were some programmes that I did – like The Ronnie Corbett Show, Crackerjack *or* Blankety Blank – *which people didn't talk about much. But if I did some stupid half-joke on* Tiswas *on a Saturday morning, all manner of people would quote it back to me the following week. If I'd realised then how good* Tiswas *was, I would have tried to be better earlier. It had such a wide-ranging effect on its target audience that even now taxi drivers, doctors, lawyers, nurses, firemen, police officers all stop me and make a point of saying, 'That bit on* Tiswas *where you sawed Sally in half was genius.'*

The thing I liked most about being on the show was the idea of being in a gang. Like the Grazebrook Crew in Dudley, the fact that I had back-up was irreplaceable. I could get a second opinion about something – a bit, a joke, a voice. Unlike being in the clubs, when I worked with the Tiswas *posse I wasn't alone. My colleagues were around me, encouraging me to do the best I could, and if it wasn't going well, taking the piss out of me as I struggled with the material. Live on air.*

Working for Tarrant – alongside Bob Carolgees, Sally, Gormo and the rest – was a welcome release from the trials and tribulations of being in the Minstrels' show, and I'll always be grateful to him.

MAMA

My mama did not disappear from my life altogether once I was on television – sometimes she was on there with me! She appeared on *Tiswas*: there was a fake *This Is Your Life* skit in which Chris Tarrant stuck what looked like a dead ferret on his head, spoke in a terrible Irish accent (in homage to Eamonn Andrews) and made up really bad jokes about his guest. He'd done it for John Gorman and Spit the Dog, so it had to be my turn at some point. And suddenly, here he was, popping out from behind a bush and surprising me (I had no idea this was going to happen):

'Lenny Henry, man of mystery, star of stage, screen and tele-phone, you first appeared on television's *New Faces*, and God knows how, but you managed to win, to eke out a pathetic career and to carve out a place in the nation's hearts . . . You had no idea, but this mornin', Lenny Henry, THIS IS YER LOIFE!'

There'd be loads of jokes about how crap I was, about my clumsiness on camera, about me nearly choking from shaving foam and passing out, and then coming to with the Nolan Sisters looking down on me with great pity in their eyes . . .

And then Tarrant looks at me and says:

'And here to tell us more about him is . . . Lenny's mum!'

We're live on TV, and I'm looking at him as if to say, 'This is a joke, right? Is Frank Carson going to come out here with an Afro wig or something?'

Suddenly, my mama walks out onto the *Tiswas* set, takes a seat and starts talking about me, with Tarrant guiding her through the questions. I don't remember what she said. All I could think was, 'MY MUM'S ON LIVE TV!'

This wasn't the real *This Is Your Life* show, so there was no real danger of Mama revealing anything too embarrassing.

However, my heart did flutter throughout, as I prayed that she wouldn't bring up hitting me in the face with a frying pan or throwing a chair at me . . .

I was relieved when it was over. I think she enjoyed herself; it was as if appearing on live television was the most natural thing in the world. That's probably where I got the whole 'Don't mind being on live telly' attitude. The mango doesn't fall very far from the tree.

Later on, she would go to various shows and come backstage, though she didn't enjoy seeing me in the clubs because of the cigarette smoke and the proximity of liquor. Her Christianity took precedence, and she would politely decline invitations to Blazers in Windsor or Caesar's Palace in Luton.

She did show up when I performed at the Night Out in Birmingham. The Night Out was one of the country's foremost cabaret venues, a massive cavern of a place with a thousand tables, each one carrying a tiny pink lampshade. Meals were provided in a basket, and there was a live band and a glitzy compère. Mama loved coming to watch me there; in her mind, it felt like I'd arrived in show business. It didn't matter that we'd come from just down the road in Dudley; the Night Out was a proper show business venue, not some disco or working men's club.

That night I had to step in for Tommy Cooper, who had gone AWOL. I did a *terrible* show. It was too daunting, too far out of my comfort zone. You couldn't see the audience, just all these little pink lampshades. To all intents and purposes, this was the big league, but for me it was way too early. I needed more experience, more stage time, more direction . . .

THE FOUR BUCKETEERS

By the time *Tiswas* ended in 1982, we knew that a new show was in the offing. Tarrant had been doing solo gigs for a while, cashing in on the programme's popularity with students by doing shows filled with party games involving pies, nudity and buckets of water. During the final series, he began touting the idea of a group version of his solo outings, calling his gang the Four Bucketeers – Chris, Bob Carolgees and Spit the dog, John Gorman and Sally James. I was an honorary bucketeer and would show up whenever I could. They made an album that featured 'The Bucket of Water Song' ('This is the song we lovers of water sing') and 'Water Is Wonderful'.

John's experience in the chart-topping group the Scaffold gave him authority in the studio, and he wrote the songs' melodies and showed us how to sing them. 'The Bucket of Water Song' charted, and the guys got to be on *Top of the Pops*. However, the BBC's health-and-safety rules being what they were meant that they couldn't throw real water at each other or the audience.

Rock-concert promoter Phil McIntyre came up with the idea of a '*Tiswas* Live' experience, featuring the Four Bucketeers and special guests. Chris and co. began slipping off at weekends to do 'golden wheelbarrow'-type gigs, where they needed said wheelbarrow to carry all the money home. I was invited to Bishop's Stortford to do a gig. I don't think I'd quite realised just how big *Tiswas* had become. We were in a venue that could safely hold about five hundred people, yet there were at least eight hundred punters crammed in and more than three hundred dissatisfied wannabes milling around outside. The stage was a hastily assembled affair made up of two big tables and some crates – an accident waiting to happen. The show itself was a hodge-podge of party games and the hit record, 'The Bucket of Water Song'. It was brilliant. I made an appearance as Algernon and performed the 'Algernon Wants You to Say "Okay!"' song. Trevor McDonut was in the house too. It was absolutely superb being on stage with the *Tiswas* posse. It was like being in a band, but covered in shaving foam – genius!

Bishop's Stortford was a triumph, but Stockport was the revelation. As we drove up to the venue, we saw a long line of people queuing up outside. There were kids, of course, running around like hyperactive doppelgangers demanding entry, but there were also lots and lots of grown-ups: students, nurses, teachers, Hell's Angels, heavy-metal fans, mods, rockers, Teds – you name it, they were there. When we got inside, we were surprised to learn that the house was full and the majority of the punters stacked up outside would not be able to get a seat. Phil McIntyre later told me that it was that show that convinced him that comedy was about to become more profitable than rock 'n' roll. I had never had a reaction like it. It was akin to my first appearance on *New Faces*. The audience were fanatical, maniacal, screaming, yelling and shouting. I think it was this response that finally gave me the courage to quit the Black and White Minstrels. Why would I stay with them when you could get reactions like this?

My experience on *Tiswas* was glorious and would prepare me for the next stage in my career – and it was all thanks to Frank Carson. So I jumped.

SIX AND THEN *THREE OF A KIND*

My time on *Tiswas* encompassed my transition away from the Black and White Minstrels' summer season and winter shows, as well as the move from working men's clubs to the big cabaret venues and theatres like the Wolverhampton Grand and the Colston Hall in Bristol. I was growing up fast and taking some knocks along the way, but finally things were panning out.

I had told Robert Luff that I no longer wanted to be connected with the Minstrels. After the Bournemouth shows and any remaining one-night stands, I was out. He was saddened that I wanted to jump ship, but once he heard my reasons, he totally understood. Our arrangement, although not contractually binding, was based on a handshake and could be terminated at any point. It was only by becoming more mature that I saw that I needed to get the hell out of Dodge.

Meanwhile, back in Birmingham at the *Cheapest Show on the Telly*, we ploughed through two series that did reasonably well when shown on BBC Midlands, triggering a response from the BBC's main HQ, where the commissioners who had seen it decided they wanted to co-opt Don Maclean and me for a new show called *Six of a Kind*.

This was a huge opportunity. The BBC gave us a pilot, with Ernest Maxin in the hot seat as producer and inspirational centre. Ernest was a live-wire producer with a pugnacious, boxer-like appearance and a low-centre-of-gravity swagger to his walk. He displayed a Gene Kelly-style confidence and could sing, dance, sell a punchline . . . the works. He knew how to make light entertainment for television, having been the producer of *The Morecambe and Wise Show*, where he was responsible for all those wonderful moments – the 'Singing in the Rain' sketch, the 'There Is Nothing Like a Dame' parody, the stripper routine in the kitchen. He was the light entertainment golden boy at the BBC, and now he was in charge of creating a brand-new variety show for the main channel, with a cast of up-and-coming talent.

My feeling now is that the show was too much, too late. There were six of us: the gorgeous black chanteuse Pearly Gates; the northern powerhouse Leah Bell, who was like a late-twentieth-century Gracie Fields; Karen Kay (Jamiroquai's mother), a superb impressionist with perfect pitch who could sing and dance and who did a brilliant Barbra Streisand, Cleo Laine and many more; Don Maclean, our principal comedian;

David Copperfield, from Doncaster, our resident knockabout comic, but also a talented musician and singer. And me.

Although it was lovely to be all lumped together like this, we knew we were doomed before we'd even started. They didn't consult us on what we actually wanted to do in the show; there was no sense of collaboration. Ernest had big ideas for numbers, dance routines and so on, but the comedy was of the 'six old people on holiday and they argue' variety. There was no room for stand-up or character comedy, so the comics (Don, David, Karen and I) all felt a little diminished.

In the meantime, Ernest was getting us to sing six-part harmonies and perform tributes to the American South with 'I Wish I Was in Dixie'. Pearly Gates and I cracked gags about how 'If we was in Dixie, we'd be swinging from a tree or some shit.' Ernest didn't mind the odd joke (he had worked with Morecambe and Wise after all), but he would get grumpy if we were having *too much* fun and not applying ourselves. David and I did a boxing sketch in which the rhythm of me doing bag work became an excuse for me to bust moves in a Fred Astaire style. Ernest made us sit on six tall stools and sing 'Feelings'. David was so funny during this that I just could not keep a straight face. Ernest was cross with us sometimes. Why couldn't we take things seriously?

In the end a BBC strike did for us. We came into work one day and there was a picket line. None of us would cross it, so we all went home. That was that. The next thing, Robert Luff was being called in to Television Centre to discuss the future of *Six of a Kind*, and what they might do instead. He and the BBC's head of entertainment, Robin Nash, discussed the idea of me and David working together, possibly alongside a female talent, on a show called *Three of a Kind*. It was no reflection on any-one in *Six of a Kind*, but the general consensus was that a cast of six performers, no matter how talented individually, felt too cumbersome and not really representative of what was going on in comedy at that particular moment.

THE ZEITGEIST

While I was transitioning from *Tiswas* to *Three of a Kind*, the Comedy Store opened in May 1979, offering more anarchic, left-leaning performers and material. A turf war was being fought between younger, more anarchic comics and their more conservative predecessors. It was an important transition. The old-school comics had been mining the same old seam – mother-in-law jokes, stories where minorities were the butt of the joke. Alternative comedy, in this first instance, was an attempt to create humour that was more inward-looking. Alexei Sayle was the Comedy Store's first MC, and he would take the piss out of the middle class and the dope-smoking left. He had various characters: a cockney mod, for example, or a journalist for *What's On in Stoke Newington* (basically a big piece of paper with 'F*ck all' written on it).

Alexei was the first superstar of alternative comedy. You only have to watch his performance on the Amnesty International film *The Secret Policeman's Other Ball* to see the influence he had on other emerging comedians. The jokes were no longer about minorities, wives and girlfriends, travelling salesmen or landladies; they were about growing up in Wales, being a student, not being able to maintain an erection, not losing your virginity and not being very good at activism.

People created a new language and new characters. Pauline Melville was brilliant at this, as was Rik Mayall. He could make you laugh just by raising an eyebrow and saying, 'What?' Adrian Edmondson was energy on legs. He made self-harming on stage look really easy to do.

What I didn't know was that I was about to be hurled into

this world of alternative comedy, which brought with it new relationships, a new TV series and a new life. Who would I be now? It was all to come, and I couldn't wait. I leapt.

Who Am I #17

This is me and my mama. It's early on in my career. Mama seems very relaxed with it all. I'm showing my teeth and my hair's every which way. One of the reasons I look confused is because at this point our relationship was changing. From the moment I began to get attention from the media, I think she realised, quite cleverly, that from now on she would have to treat me differently. She did not interfere with my contracts or choice of shows. She was broadly encouraging and was available to take lots of pictures and talk to the press when called upon to do so. In my brain, when she walked on Tiswas and took part in a spoof This Is Your Life, to much hilarity amid the caged and uncaged members of the audience, I kept having flashbacks of Mama hitting me in the face with a frying pan.

It took a while for me to accept this new version, and of course in the end, when she was prepared to talk about her struggle to leave Jamaica, set up home here and raise a family in a hostile environment, I began to understand her predicament. This is a nice photo. I wish we'd been like that for longer. (Getty)

Afterword

And so it ends – but there's more of my story to come. I didn't intend to finish at that particular point, but it just felt like it was the right moment to hit the 'Pause' button before going off on another 100,000-word jam session on the life and times of Lenny Henry, c.1980 to the present day. Writing a memoir plunges you back into places you may not want to revisit, smack dab into the past, where all those monsters and ghouls still lurk, ready to scour your soul with emotional Brillo Pads.

It's time to bid farewell: to my mama, my papa and my brother Hylton; to the clubs, cabarets and entertainment palaces of my youth; and to you, my gentle reader. What this exercise has taught me is that we do stand on the shoulders of giants. People achieve their dreams by relying on the advice and support of their elders, betters and predecessors. And I am no different. I am the sum of my enthusiasms, obsessions, tastes and weaknesses.

So here I am back in the taxi where it all started, and I'm wondering if I'd change any aspect of this first section of my life. All the hard knocks that assailed me as I fell through the tree of life: hidden origins, racism, fighting at school, integration, mates, nurturing, winning *New Faces*, losing *New Faces*, the Black and White Minstrels, meeting all those great people in clubland, learning how to put together a set, figuring out why 1970s-style clubland comedy wasn't really my bag, the complete joy of children's television and being hit repeatedly by buckets of water and custard pies thrown by a rather large man in a black leotard.

Of course, the answer is no. It had been a hell of a life . . . but there was much more to come.

Notes to a Young Comic

I didn't know I was going to be a comedian. I was too busy impersonating teachers, friends, actors from movies and comedians from television. I was a consumer first. When I was starting out, there was no Obi-Wan Kenobi figure to lead me to the comedy Death Star. I was on my own. Now, having worked as a comedian for over thirty years, I thought it might be pertinent to pass on some stuff about performance, stand-up and the rest. I hope that some of what follows may come in useful to you if you're a young aspiring comic.

1. Be a Fan, a Customer, a Consumer

Most of the people you talk to in the UK business have stories about listening to *The Goon Show* on the radio, or watching *Monty Python* and learning all the sketches off by heart, or watching Peter Cook and Dudley Moore, or listening to shows like *Round the Horne* or *Hancock's Half Hour*. It helps to be a fan because you're making a choice: you're figuring out what your taste in comedy might be, and by choosing to be a fan, you're immersing yourself in different types of writing and performance.

Spike Milligan's bravura run as creator and chief writer of *The Goon Show* led to several nervous breakdowns, but he also called upon his co-creators – Peter Sellers, Harry Secombe, Eric Sykes, Larry Stephens, Maurice Wiltshire, John Antrobus – to assist with the continuing process of moulding the bizarre logic of that insane universe. Listening to them and the way they play with time, surprise and voices, you get the sense that Milligan's methodology was to riff and improvise comedically, like the jazz musician he actually was. Watching the Pythons is another story, six brains in service to unified ideas: organised chaos, no punchlines, multiple characters and an animation style that crossed classical Greek imagery with Victorian postcard smut. The Pythons mixed the intellectual with the mundane, visual slapstick (just think of the Ministry of Silly Walks) with the articulate set-up and punch, the straight-forward sketch (such as 'The Argument') with the impossible premise (as in 'Summarise Proust'). They were all great performers too. You're buying into something when you admit to a liking for a particular style of comedy.

Dave Allen was a storyteller and an aspiring actor. His stories were always coloured with ornamentations and skilful illustration, whereas someone like Steven Wright, the dazed and confused, stumbling Boston comic with the appearance of an acid casualty but the mind of a rocket scientist, makes every joke a kind of haiku:

I bought some dehydrated water, but I don't know what to add.

Each Steven Wright joke is like a mini-sketch, his delivery a kind of mumbled, semi-apologetic drone that belies the work that has gone into the construction of each routine.

I have a half-twin. I also have a Siamese stepson.

This is a mind/thought process of which an audience desperately wants to be a part.

There have always been genre comedians: Hope and Crosby with their road adventures; Abbott and Costello and their frenzied encounters with werewolves, Dracula and Frankenstein's monster. Compare this to the League of Gentlemen's extremely detailed horror comedy.

So being a consumer is important, because even though you might not know what you're doing, your constant drinking from the well of *The Young Ones* or *French and Saunders* or *Goodness Gracious Me* or *Saturday Night Live* or *Beyond the Fringe* or *Hancock's Half Hour* means you're making a choice. You're editing continually. And with those choices you're nailing your colours to the mast for the future.

2. Know the Difference Between Being Funny and Telling Jokes

I've never really got on with jokes. I like them, but as a laughter delivery mechanism there's an element of dissatisfaction about them that I've never quite been able to shake off. They're old-fashioned. A man walks into a bar . . . I went to the doctor the other day . . . An Englishman, Irishman and a Scotsman . . . Two blondes walking down the street . . . A Jamaican guy stops at the traffic lights . . . I knocked on the door, a Pakistani bloke answered it . . .

As you make your way through the hundreds and hundreds of jokes available online or in dusty old books, there's a feeling of victimisation about a lot of the material. Someone has to be the butt of these jokes (the Irishman, the Pakistani, the Jamaican, the blonde, the gay guy, the lesbian, the Jew, sometimes the disabled person). There's no level playing field here; someone's going to get a kicking. It's as if joke-tellers are in a heightened position when they do their thing. They are superior, always the observer, always the person pointing out the stupid thing that the minority/unfortunate individual did or said. Some of these jokes are really harmful.

When Bernard Manning used to say about his Pakistani/

Irish/Jamaican-type jokes that 'It's just a bit of fun,' or, 'If people can't take a joke . . .', it must have been difficult to be in the audience and not feel victimised. Don Rickles, the Las Vegas comic who regularly roasted Mexicans, Jews, Poles and so on, walked the same path. There's something a bit miserable and bullying about this type of comedy. If I go out to see some comedy, I don't want to be shat on from a great height.

Much as I respect some of the old-school comedians, I find myself preferring people who can do something else. Someone told me yonks ago that it's really important to do things that the audience can't do, and that has always stuck with me. If all you're doing is telling a joke – 'A man walked into a bar . . .' – then you're basically repeating something that anybody could do.

The big battle is deciding whether you're going to be a funny person or whether you're going to tell jokes. Groucho Marx had fantastic one-liners:

They had to pull you down and put up a building in your place.

A child of five could understand this. Send someone to get me a five-year-old kid – I can't make head nor tail of this.

Go, and never darken my towels again.

I've had a perfectly wonderful evening. But this wasn't it.

All funny one-liners, but Groucho also walked funny, talked funny, looked funny and sang funny. Everything he did was funny. That's the challenge for all comedians. It's one thing to stand there and churn out old jokes; it's a completely different kettle of fish to come on stage and communicate with every tool you have at your disposal, to be prepared to do anything with voice, movement, costume, dynamics and tension to get laughs.

Lee Evans, Jerry Lewis, Robin Williams, Richard Pryor, Steve Martin, Lily Tomlin, French and Saunders, Rik Mayall, Alexei

Sayle, Kevin Hart and Sarah Silverman all seem to be willing to park the notion of the strictly verbal short-story form in favour of characterisation, visual humour and general silliness. The commitment to an all-encompassing funny vibe pays off better in the long run. As many people have pointed out, Steve Martin presented himself as 'showbiz incarnate', which is a complicated way of saying that he pretended he was doing the best show you'd ever seen while wearing an arrow through the head, making balloon animals and juggling pretend kittens.

Richard Pryor migrated from doing routines and jokes in the style of Bill Cosby to presenting stories and anecdotes from his life in the most honest way he could, like a forensic documentarian. Many people have followed in his footsteps. I'm not sure I'd be brave enough to do that. It takes a huge amount of courage to embark on a style and structure that means that everything that comes out of your mouth and is displayed by the movement of your body must be as honest as it can possibly be.

Being funny means going with the flow, reading the room, picking up on what's going on, not just sticking to the script. It's dangerous, but it can lead somewhere. It can be incredibly funny and true.

I recently got into Charlie Chaplin. I was on tour, and a friend of mine recommended that I take the opportunity to watch a couple of Chaplin films. I shrieked in horror. I'd always found *The Tramp* to be cloyingly sentimental. Chaplin was too involved in his dancer's physicality, and there were not enough jokes. But on rewatching I found in Chaplin a total commitment to storytelling, to encapsulating comedy and tragedy. He was whip-smart and ingeniously balletic when performing physical comedy. There's a moment of heart-stopping bravura in *Modern Times* when he roller-skates blindfold, showboating for the object of his desire, skating ever more precariously towards a hole in the floor.

WHO AM I, AGAIN?

Being a funny person means you perhaps tend more to spontaneity than to rigid structures. You might start off with an hour's template, but once you've learnt it and know where all the laughs are, the funny person's inclination is to play with the text and the structure to see what happens. The traditionalist will stick to the same wording/structure/rigidity for the entire lifetime of that routine.

This is a story against me now. I saw a comedian at the Improv in LA in the early 1980s. She was very funny and had a routine about being on a roller-coaster ride in Florida, where 'you went forwards in a loop-the-loop, and then came backwards at speed through your own vomit'. I loved that joke and may even have borrowed it from time to time. Imagine my horror when, six years later, I revisited that nightclub and saw the same comedian hit the stage. She did a couple of topical things, and then launched straight into a well-practised and honed routine about roller coasters. Word-for-word came the thing about the vomit. I had to quickly explain to my girlfriend that this was the person I'd nicked that joke from. Shame was heaped on me that night, and I vowed never to borrow material again. But in a wider sense this was a perfect illustration of the joke-teller versus funny person argument. This comedian had shaped and crafted a twenty-minute set from which she hadn't veered for six years! Where was the fluidity, the variety, the experimentation?

When I was doing stand-up, I had a very strict structure, but I would always improvise around it whenever the opportunity arose. I loved the feeling and confidence of doing material that worked unfailingly, but I also loved the idea of playing with an audience. To mine a particular seam for comedy gold whenever possible is not only a way of generating material, but also a way of keeping yourself on your toes. No question, the text is important, and the honing of one-liners is a basic tenet of stand-up survival, but to a funny person with comedy bones the well-honed/crafted joke is like when they do a serving suggestion in a magazine – it looks great on the page, but it might come out very different in performance.

And the performance is everything.

3. Performance: What I Want from a Comedian

When I go and see a comic, I want structure. You don't pay all that money for a ramshackle mess, some dude having a nervous breakdown on stage and repeatedly saying, 'Err . . . that got a huge laugh last night. I don't know what's the matter with you guys. Why do you even bother to come out? OK, this next bit usually sets the bar for what kind of an audience you're going to be. If you don't laugh at this, you're scum . . .' etc., etc. On the other hand, you also don't want Mr Set-Up Punch reciting jokes in a bored monotone, with exactly the same pauses, tics, twitches and embellishment that they had on day one.

I'm looking for something else: either the attempt to speak honestly and from the heart, with smart intelligence and physicality; or the attempt to tell an enormous story with very few resources, like Patrick Barlow and Jim Broadbent in the National Theatre of Brent, or the kind of performer who says, 'Hey, we're going this way,' and then completely wrong-foots you and takes you all the way to a place you didn't ever want to go to.

In the last few years I've learnt that acquiring the skills of timing, endurance, memory, improvisation and structure – and questioning all of those things with your performance – is the big brass ring for a performer. Question everything with every aspect of your performance, maintain honesty as much as you can. Don't just monitor the audience, but also your performance and that of your colleagues.

The main thing I want from a performance is the sense that anything can happen, that the performer can go anywhere, do anything, unhindered by structure or text. This, as Robin Williams found during his stint in *Waiting for Godot*, is tough, but achievable. I think Williams, Jack Nicholson, Russell Brand, Amy Schumer, John Belushi, Richard Pryor and Will Ferrell all have this quality.

But if you want to be a comedian, you have to ask yourself whether you want to tell jokes or whether you want to be the joke. That's all you need to be thinking about.

4. Craft

The recently deceased Sir Ken Dodd was not only a genius-level comedian, but a student of comedy, a funnyman who encapsulated an articulate verbal flow, a ridiculous and colourful appearance, an artful manipulation of hair, buck-teeth and a barrage of double entendres. Doddy also sang, perhaps in the canny knowledge that non-stop gags can sometimes be too much of a good thing. He had books and books of jokes, whether overheard, received in good faith for free or paid for. However, Doddy's almost unerring eye for the naughty McGill's postcard-style punchline, as well as for the well-crafted topical gag, meant that he never went out of vogue. Although he might have become more conservative in his old age, his appearance, wit, style and mode of attack meant that he was never boring.

When he came to your town he'd always done a bit of research and would deftly cock a snook at any particular aspect of the town that its inhabitants were proud of. Doddy's craft, the sense that he had worked on this material without pause, was never really evident to his audience. They were too busy laughing. And that's my point. All the work he put in, that all us comedians put in – collecting jokes, writing down funny thoughts in one's journal, practising silly walks in the park when you think no one's looking, trying out routines on open-mic spots, casually slipping material into conversations with friends and family and watching their response – all of these things are legitimate actions for someone who wants to be funny professionally.

For many years Doddy had a lady who came to every performance and marked in a book which jokes went really well that night, which did OK and which ones tanked. She had been doing this for years, and if Doddy so desired, she could go back five years to when they were last in that town and see which jokes had gone down well that night. She was, in fact, a one-person focus group.

It's really important to have some system that judges the impact of your material, whether you tape it, listen back afterwards and make notes or a close friend makes notes during the performance. This kind of input is invaluable. Nobody tells you this stuff when you start out. However, within a couple of years I discovered that all the older comics were desperate to share information about craft and performance.

So I would advise young comics to go to comedy clubs – a lot. Watch the comedians, get a sense of who they are. When they've finished, get up the courage to talk to them after the show. Ask them questions about what you just saw. I'm sure they'll be happy to fill you in on technique, writing, mic control and hydration – especially if you buy them a drink. All of those things are important, but it's up to you to find out why.

Bob Monkhouse was similar to Doddy. He collected joke books and had a wide-ranging understanding of joke structure. He approached me once at a BBC light entertainment party and quoted my characters back at me:

'Yes, PC Ganja, very good. "Good evening, my name is PC Ganja. This my dog, Selassie."'

Or he'd do Delbert:

'The policeman pulled me over. He put his head through the window. Then I wound it down. That must've hurt.'

He knew everybody's jokes and routines. I've heard rumours that he taped American comedy shows from the wireless when he was a young boy, and in adulthood kept journals of almost every comedy show he'd ever seen, taking particular note of his favourite gags and the comics who told them.

Bob's attention to craft regularly spilled over into performance and was boosted by his immense confidence. I would often watch him and wish that I had his attention to detail. Although he wasn't everybody's cup of tea, I always thought he was supremely professional. He had always done his homework – which is what craft is, I guess. In the way that chefs know that only a certain type of pan is acceptable in a proper kitchen, and mechanics realise you need the right tools for the right jobs, comedy performers understand that there are many approaches to their craft, but there are key tools they will need for their particular journey.

Jerry Seinfeld sits down and wrestles with subject matter and premises for a couple of hours every day without fail. (It's worth watching his 2002 DVD *Comedian* to glean an insight into his process.) Richard Pryor would go woodshedding at the Comedy Store. He'd get up on stage late at night and start riffing on whatever subject came to mind to see if it was worth pursuing. Robin Williams would film all day and then go out at night looking for a comedy venue that would allow him to get up on stage. Tommy Cooper collected stupid tricks and would spend weeks crafting a silly narrative that would allow him to do that stupid trick on stage. I would sit in my dressing room listening to the audience on the intercom, while writing a journal about my journey to that venue, some of which would be included in the opening ten minutes of the show.

Our habits lead to our craft. It could be as simple as ring-fencing five minutes of every show – or more, if you're brave – to riff on whatever subject you choose. Ben Elton would start a new tour by performing big chunks of the previous one, while incrementally adding new bits as he went along, until the new material had eventually shafted the old.

If this sounds like a lot of work to you, you're absolutely right. But if you want to be really good, then it's worth investing some time. It's worth hunkering down and watching all of your favourite comedians online, in chunks, to see if there's any connective tissue between what they do and what you'd like to. Craft is everything, and coupled with your instinct, it could lead somewhere very profitable indeed. Not just in terms of money – although that is a consideration – but in terms of job satisfaction. Who doesn't want that?

5. Mindset

You've got to get your mind right before you perform, in the same way as you've got to get your mind right before you write. Are you a solitary person? Do you need utter silence and tranquillity before you can slip onto the runway in order to taxi before take-off? I like sitting in my dressing room listening to quiet music, making notes and slowly gearing up for the performance. The music gets louder and thumpier the nearer to the performance I get.

I used to like tinkly music, candles and solitude when writing, but now I find that peace and quiet and some company in the other room or nearby seem conducive to a better way of working. A deadline helps: the nearer you get, the harder you have to work to produce. And a critical friend to help you discern the wheat from the chaff comes in very handy indeed.

There are some people who like an entourage, one or two people whose job it is to 'fluff' them to the extent that they can go on stage and kill because they've been cracking gags with their pals all day leading up to this moment. I once saw a comedian in New York who showed up with his four mates, talking loudly at the bar, and then when he was introduced on stage he continued the conversation he'd been having with his friends at the mic! They'd shout out to him, 'Yo, dude, do dat shit about yo' mama,' and he would!

It seemed to work for him, but writing with an entourage is a bit trickier. Who owns the intellectual property at the end of the day? You couldn't really say you'd written it on your own.

Victoria Wood would sit at her kitchen table and basically grind it out day after day, year after year. Whether it was routines, jokes, songs or plays, she sat down on her own and did the work. This method can bear fruit if you have a strong work ethic and a determination to get it done. There's a saying: 'Don't get it right, just get it written.' If you sit down every day and write for two hours, you're going to come up with something. It's just a matter of making sure you get the right feedback when you need it. And you *will* need it.

I used to make lots of lists before a performance, because at that point there are two ways to go: either meditate right up until the beginning of the show, so that you're not thinking about the show at all; or make lists! My list-making could range from writing out in note form every routine in the show to remind myself of its shape and content, to trying to reduce the show to ten bullet points. Or I could fill the pre-show zone with yoga, or shoulder and neck massages, or singing drills. Whatever I do, there's a sense that it's all leading into the show.

The needier performers tend to have the promoter and a dog and a child and a best mate and a parent hanging out with them in the dressing room right up until show time. I saw somebody in Edinburgh whose huge dog began the show on stage and then wandered on and off at various moments whenever it suited him. It was a bit distracting.

Whichever method you choose, bear in mind that at the beginning/open-mic stage, you might not have a dressing room or a space in which to prepare. A lot of places make you wait by the bar or sit in the room during someone else's performance. This can be frightening. I was never very good at it because if you're about to follow someone who has just slayed the audience, even to the point where the staff are banging on tables and saying, 'Stop! Please!' you might feel you owe it to yourself to step outside, climb into an Uber and go home, vowing never to return.

Whenever I was in New York, I would either stand in the reception or the foyer, or if possible, ask someone to give me a three-minute warning so that I could enter the venue when I was ready, rather than having to endure Mr or Mrs Comedy Genius Pants in the preceding slot.

It's tricky to get your set together in the midst of meals and drinks being served, heckling, bravura stand-up, gut-busting laughter. If there's any kind of meditation process you can train yourself to do, this is the place to deploy it. Don't let yourself get rattled.

A fellow comedian told me that if someone was on just before her and they had brought the house down, it was her job to walk on after them and use their energy and what they'd done with the room. She would acknowledge how good they'd been, but she would also carefully prepare the way for her own material, so that it was as clunk-free as possible. She would refer to their material or to an audience member who might have had the piss taken out of them; or if the comic had roasted a particular movie, she might comment on that movie too. All are survival techniques.

If, by necessity, you have to be in the room before it's your turn to take to the stage, then take this opportunity to read the room and make a mental map of the kinds of things the audience are laughing at.

Some comics make a point of homing in on a comic from out of town and chatting to them in a genial 'mine host' kind of way in order to try out their material. I remember having a fantastic conversation with a Canadian comic at the Montreal Comedy Festival. It was as though he'd just decided that I was going to be his best friend. He chatted and chatted and chatted, made lots and lots and lots of jokes. I roared with laughter and felt special. And then the bastard went on stage and repeated that entire conversation to the audience, who dutifully laughed in all the same places I'd laughed. He was rehearsing his act on me, which is the comedy equivalent of a dog dry-humping your leg.

So meditation in the dressing room, list-making, yoga, some form of exercise, music, writing or . . . total immersion in the room you're about to play.

6. What to Wear

When you're starting out, it's important not to overdress. At the open-mic stage, a lot of comedians walk on in whatever they happen to be wearing at that moment, and even when you're at the three-shows-a-night-'cos-the-cash-is-pretty-decent stage, unless it's a particular affectation of yours to wear a tuxedo and a bow tie, a general rule of thumb is: wear the clothes in which you're comfortable.

At the beginning of his career Robin Williams looked like he was fresh from the *commedia dell'arte* or mime school. He wore berets, loose-fitting tracksuit bottoms and garishly coloured sweaters or T-shirts. He looked like he was in one long continuous improv class, which is perhaps why his performances were so loose and Hydra-headed. Robin always looked ready for anything and was dressed down so that if he had to roll around on the floor or climb the scenery, it wouldn't matter so much if he tore something or got grubby. His comedy at that point was experimental, improvisational, which demanded an informality. No suits allowed.

However, some venues stipulate that performers dress to a certain standard. If you were booked for cabaret or a theatre performance in the late 1970s/early '80s, you were expected to wear a suit and tie and shiny shoes. You couldn't go on scruffy, or else the promoter or stage manager would tell you off. Max Bygraves once told me: 'When you walk on stage, take the applause and give 'em a minute. Let 'em see the suit.'

I have to admit that from the very early days of my career, I equated being on stage with dressing nicely. I always wanted to look good on stage, and only later, after I'd seen the Comic Strip, did I think that I could get away with wearing a leather jacket and a pair of jeans.

Steve Martin's white suit hinted at what journalist Nathan Heller calls his 'buttoned-up-but-libertine, childlike-but-arrantly-adult routine'. Steve wore the white suit so he could be seen beyond the first twenty rows at an arena gig. I think he also wore it to look cool. There was a sense that he was pandering to the more conservative crowd, while also sneakily preaching to the hipsters. As Heller says, 'One moment he seemed to be trying to force the sixties back into their box. A second later, he was sucking on his balloons to get high.'

Billy Connolly at his peak, on the other hand, looked like a Hell's Angel or a rock star: big shaggy hair, tights, Doc Martens, baggy leopard-skin shirt. It was a statement. He was an alien; he wasn't one of us. He carried a guitar, which in folky terms meant, 'Oh, he is like us. He just dresses like a weirdo.' Jasper Carrott wasn't as out there as Billy back in the day, but he had a look: long hair, rugby shirt, jeans, trainers. It was an anti-showbiz appearance that said, 'I'm not one of those cabaret guys.'

Don Maclean took me to his tailor when I was starting out. I was just about to embark on my first summer season with the Black and White Minstrels. This was in the mid-1970s. I admired Don's stage clothes. He looked slick, sometimes in a black tuxedo and floppy bow tie, other times in well-pressed beige or sky-blue cotton or velvet, with flares and patent leather shoes. His tailor measured me up for three suits, all of which gave the impression that I was a forty-something club comic. To the Minstrels' audience, I looked like a seasoned performer from 1970s UK clubland. But now when I see those pictures, I can't help thinking that I look ridiculous. I was seventeen, of Afro-Caribbean descent, and loved going clubbing and wearing clothes that reflected my age, musical tastes and class. I usually wore Oxford bags, tank tops, loafers and shirts with the rounded collars. Why, then, was I dressed like a depressed middle-aged northern club comic? Only when I was free of the Minstrels, summer season and pantomime, and beginning to explore elements of the alternative comedy world, did I begin to think that there was another way to present myself on stage.

When you're on stage, you have to be able to sweat, move, dance, do whatever you want. If your clothes don't allow you to perform to the best of your ability, then, as Jay-Z says, 'just change clothes'.

7. Mic Technique

The mic is there to help you. It is not there to be eaten, to bang your head against, to perform elaborate sexual jokes with or anything else. It is there to magnify your voice and help you to be heard by most of the audience.

However, a skilled comedian will often use the microphone to make sound effects. Bill Cosby was into this. Listening to his albums, his use of dynamics and sound effects (cars, martial arts-style hits, pouring water, glugging down alcohol, etc.) is a master-class in storytelling. As someone who listened to Cosby albums from the mid-1970s, I was very aware as a young comic that using the mic as a tool to enhance your comedy was a no-brainer.

But there are some things you have to consider. Would you use a microphone that somebody else has breathed all over on stage? Would you use a microphone that your predecessor has just simulated oral sex with or rubbed all over their body? Lots of comedians put the mic in their mouth, beatbox with it very close to their lips, or lick or spit on it. My advice is, if you're going to be that kind of comic, then buy your own mic. Plenty of people do, and it saves your fellow comedians from having to confront your oral hygiene, or lack thereof, mid-performance.

Because of hip-hop culture, there's a lot of mic dropping going on at the end of performances. If you're using somebody else's mic, don't do that, or else find a way to drop the mic without slamming it to the ground and thus damaging its internal workings. Otherwise, you may end up with a bill.

8. The Grind

It goes on and on till the break of dawn. The grind is a state of mind. It's all about the work, and if you don't get it now, you never will.

My favourite grinding inspiration is Rocky Balboa – that moment when he realises he better get his groove on if he's going to challenge the greatest heavyweight champion there has ever been, Apollo Creed. So he gets up in the morning at holy mackerel o'clock, says 'Hi' to his two pet turtles Cuff and Link, then goes to the fridge and cracks raw eggs into a container and drinks them. Then, as the sun peeps over the horizon, we see Rocky begin his morning training regime, which involves a lot of running – through the market place, down by the docks, up endless steps. By the end of it we've got the idea: training is tough; training to take on the heavyweight champion of the world is much, much, much tougher.

The point is, if you have the talent to be a comedian, grab the brass ring and run with it. But if you're not gifted with a visible comedic talent, then you're going to have to work at it. There are plenty of comics making a living who don't look or behave in a naturally funny way. These comics say funny things and have a funny attitude, but they don't slay you. They don't have that extraordinary visual comedy garnish when they act out situations. Their comedy is all from the neck up, whereas Robin Williams or Richard Pryor or Steve Martin or Lee Evans, at their height, all chose to physicalise everything they did. They certainly inspired me to move and groove on stage. I wanted to be like them and tried my hardest to act out everything I could. The grind isn't just about technique, though; there's the boredom of repeatedly getting up and doing bits whenever you can.

There's a sequence in Jerry Seinfeld's *Comedian* that is about what you do when you have to start again from scratch. The film tells the story of the aftermath of Jerry dumping all his old material into one final TV show. Now he sets himself the task of building a new show from zero, and we see him writing new bits, fiddling with them, trying them out on colleagues, flying to terrible comedy clubs, cellars and pits, just to get stage time with his new material. That's what every comedian has to do: write, rehearse, try out, edit, repeat until sick.

There's something strangely rewarding about working in a new bit. If you're a well-known comic, you get some play time – maybe two or three minutes up front – to mess around with the crowd using your old, dependable stuff, before slowly easing into the new material. If you're not well known, do your best three jokes to open, save the next funniest thing you do for a closer, and pack the middle with the new stuff. What have you got to lose?

I think if you're gifted enough to craft your own material, then go with God and craft away. However, if you're funny but

NOTES TO A YOUNG COMIC

are all over the place (like a lot of us), then you'll need a collab-orator – either a friend, colleague or director – to sit with you and listen to the material and help you make choices. Choosing what works and what doesn't is tough when you're on your own. You're fine in a troupe like the Pythons, because every-one's smart and has an opinion and wants the show to be the best it can be. You're fine in a double act like French and Saunders or Morecambe and Wise or Laurel and Hardy, because there's two of you, and one of you is going to have an opinion about exactly how the show should be. If you're on your own, you're relying mostly on the audience, so ask someone to audit the act and give you feedback. It's essential.

If you love jokes, you can work with someone who cares only about the jokes per minute ratio. They can tell you if there aren't enough or too many, or if some of them are weak or not in the right place or whatever. If you love narrative structure/shape/*coups de théâtre*, then sit with a director and create not only a safe space for you to do your thing, but also a show with a clearly delineated beginning, middle and end, correct pacing, etc. Directors tend to cost money, so get your family or friends to come and watch your show. Ask them to be brutally honest – you need that.

9. Open Mic

I talk about these a lot but haven't done many of them. They're a good way of getting a foot on the bottom rung of the stand-up ladder. They'll be in a room in a pub. Sometimes there'll be forty people, if you're lucky; other venues hold between a hundred and two hundred punters. There'll be a bar somewhere in the vicinity, which means you're going to have to deal with drink-ers and clatterers and talkers. Of course, the ideal environment for your brand-new, scorching-hot material is a place where the audience sit respectfully and laugh at every single one of your carefully crafted jokes. Most of us, though, have to deal with sneezes, coughs, involuntary screams, inappropriate comments and heckles. Audiences rarely sit still for long, and if they do sit there quietly, they invariably aren't enjoying themselves.

At your usual open mic there'll be a compère; it was probably his idea to have an open mic night in the first place. My brother Paul did it for a while. He and a couple of others researched a venue, convinced the pub landlord that he needed a comedy night and – BOOM! – suddenly there were all these people off the telly turning up to try out new material. If you're new, you will show up on the night when they allow new people to come on and do five minutes. You can't just rock up at 8.45 p.m. and expect to get a slot; you have to be respectful, ring ahead, show up ahead of time, get your name on the list.

Then there's the tricky question of 'What do I do when I get up there?' Well . . . you can just riff and storm it, but what happens the next night when you try the whole riff thing and it doesn't work? I advise that you don't riff. If you're writing stuff and there's a sequence of jokes or events or anecdotes that go down particularly well when you've tried them out on your friends or family – I'm talking things that always get laughs – then do that bit your first time out. It's an odd experience – you're trying to make complete strangers laugh.

Once you sense what the funny bits might be, really practise – the more, the better. You want to be able to spit out jokes like Drake spits out lyrics. You need to have your jokes so polished and perfect that when you get up there and it's you and the audience, you're the funniest mate they have never met before. You and the audience are having a conversation in which you're fooling around verbally or physically and they're learning about you – how your mind works, how your body jerks.

The more gigs you do, the more you get used to the audience's reaction. You'll figure out what's working and what isn't; you'll rewrite or rethink the bits that keep falling apart. Most times you'll drop them completely. Just because something didn't work doesn't mean you're not funny. You can seek advice from a co-writer or another comic who's similar to you in style. You could say, 'If you watch my act and give me notes, I'll do the same for you.' If someone starts writing good jokes for you, you might have to shell out at some point, so make sure you write down your agreement – it saves mess later.

I didn't really do any writing. I was an impressionist who did jokes, so my routines were foraged from friends, television and strangers in pubs or taxis telling me gags. The first eight years was basically me taking advantage of the fact that my predominantly white audience had never seen a black impressionist before. They seemed to like what I did most of the time. When I died, though, it was pretty brutal.

Because my first onstage appearances were me 'making it up as I went along', I tried to be different at every gig. If I'd been booked for twenty minutes or half an hour and tried to incorporate improvisation into my usual set, it just didn't work. The audience recognised the material that I'd done on television and liked it, but there was a real sense of 'Why doesn't the black kid from the telly have a proper act?'

Three of a Kind's producer, Paul Jackson, suggested that I could collaborate with Kim Fuller (*Not the Nine O'Clock News*, *Three of a Kind*, *Carrott's Lib*, *The Tracey Ullman Show*). I engaged Kim to come and watch me in cabaret a couple of times. He ascertained that I needed a stronger structure and better jokes, so we sat down and pieced together an act that was made up of characters, impressions and songs, all held together by bits of chat. That was it. We worked on it for a month and then debuted the new hour of material at a cabaret/restaurant venue in Luton. I remember getting big laughs – continuously.

It was like a dream. Kim had brought a structure and a more disciplined approach to the amount of jokes per routine. I became very dependent on this relationship throughout the 1980s and for everything I did on TV. My earliest attempts at stand-up were all made with Kim helping me to figure out the path to success.

So a writing partner is good. However, much better is trying out material at a place where you trust the audience's judgement. What I mean is, if you can find a venue where you get laughs, such that when you go to another venue you get similar laughs, then that is a relationship to cherish. Being a live act is about finding the best material and sticking to it for as long as you can. I know that seems a bit conservative – it's fine to be constantly developing – but I loved Tommy Cooper, and he hardly ever changed his act.

There's something to be said for really working your material until it shines like a jewel, so that you can do it in any condition – happy, sad, overweight, underweight, joyous, depressed as buggery. If you have an act you can do anytime, anywhere, anyhow . . . then that is a fine thing.

10. Bad Habits

On the good nights you can feel sensational – God-like almost. The audience are lovely, but they are not your friends and family. Don't treat every gig and after-party like therapy. It's alright to do your job and go home.

Don't get into the habit of having people talk to you right up to the moment when your name is announced. Some people come into your dressing room before the show and want to hang out. This is great if you know the show and are confident, but if you have *any* fears about sequence, timing, patterning or whatever, then just before the show is usually a good time to make lists, practise or move around. If you're doing a show where you don't have a dressing room, go to the toilet, find an empty cubicle and sit for five minutes. Take your time, do some deep breathing . . . then come out, wash your face and get ready. You've got a show to do.

Back in 1975 at the London Palladium, in the hiatus between rehearsals and the live final of the *New Faces* winners' show, I was literally 'bricking it' backstage in the dressing room. All my confidence had gone. I hated the jokes, the impressions, my clothes – everything. Mike Felix, a piano-playing, boogie-woogie comic, gave me some breathing exercises, and I straightened out and got through the show reasonably well. It's good to find a moment of clarity just before you go on. Get your head in the game. Maybe do like Chris Rock before an important gig: watch *Rocky* – that'll get you in the right space, if nothing else works . . .

11. Interactivity

I got into the habit of talking to the front row of the audience. It got so lengthy that in the end Ken Bowlly, my musical director, took to playing an AC/DC-style power chord on his guitar to signal 'Time to move on, Len.' Sometimes I'd be twenty-five minutes into the show. The fact is, I like talking to the audience. You can find nuggets of material you might not have discovered if you'd just gone on and done your act. However, if you have spent all that time shaping and honing and sharpening your material, do you really want to waste all that effort by deciding to 'wing it' for half an hour or so? Save the winging-it for the times when you're compèring. I want to have a playful relationship with the audience, but I also want to give them a show when the time comes.

If you're going to get people up out of the audience, it is important that the audience member agrees to be your stooge.

A quick word before they get up will do. You have to sort of guide them through the experience of being on stage with you. There are some bits where you hardly need to say anything at all, but a general rule of thumb is that you should canvass opinion about 'who wants to be in the show' before the lights go down, or just ask before you do the bit if someone would mind helping you out.

We've all seen shows where the member of the public was really funny and fitted in with everything the performer wanted, but sometimes they can freak out, and then you've got a problem on your hands. Be really careful. As Spider Man says: with great power comes great responsibility.

12. Television

When I went on television my attitude was, 'This is all or nothing.' I poured all my energy into coming up with the best three minutes I could think of. I was sixteen.

These days young comedians are much more aware of their material, of what works and what doesn't. They tend to know what routine is going to represent them in the best possible way. When a scout has seen you and reports back to their boss, they will usually show a clip from the Internet or wherever you showcase your best work. The boss will then expect something resembling your best work on their TV show. However, if the producers want you to do something similar to what they first saw, they might ask you to 're-record' one of your best bits. It's doable. I was at BBC Lime Grove sound recording studios once and Lenny Kravitz was there. The BBC said he couldn't mime to the original track of one of his own songs on *Top of the Pops*; he had to record a new track especially. Kravitz didn't moan or yell; he just got his synth, drum machine and guitar and remade the track in a couple of hours. It was brilliant. The point is, you should be able to re-present your party piece or even replicate it at the drop of a hat, if necessary.

If they come and see you live, they're going to want your best routine for the TV. If you don't mind retiring that particular bit, fine; but if you don't want to give it up just yet, you might have to negotiate something else – your opening routine or your pivotal thirty-mins-in routine. Apparently, Jay Leno has a hilarious bit about his dad trying to get the video machine to work, and he's never done it on TV. So protect your jewels until you're ready to let 'em go, and then – BAM! – do 'em on telly and get all that lovely praise and kudos.

13. The Big Break

My big break, arguably, was performing at the Queen Mary Ballroom in 1974 in front of Mike Hollis. He then wrote to *New Faces* and *Opportunity Knocks*, and the ripple effect brought me to where I am today.

Nowadays people get their break on the Internet . . . and before you know it, they've got 3 million followers. There's also the long road: working open mics, then getting booked a few nights a week, then a couple of shows a night, then getting it together to put on a show at the Edinburgh Festival, then a four- or five-star review, then a transfer to London, and then – BOOM! – someone from *8 Out of 10 Cats* or *Russell Howard's Good News* spots you and they want you to come and play . . .

The path was different back in the day. I knew that I wanted a TV show like Dave Allen's or Mike Yarwood's. Nowadays, the TV bigwigs shun the sketch show and there are no variety shows where a comedian can come on and rock for five minutes.

Although the comic-centred sketch show has gone the way of all things, there are other ways to skin a cat. Your big break may not come from a stellar appearance on a mainstream variety show like *Britain's Got Talent*, but you may get a break by being brilliant at Edinburgh or serially successful in all the pubs in your neighbourhood. Maybe a clip goes viral or you get the gig as the over-excitable weatherman on a local radio show. There are many paths to the promised land. You just have to set a goal, aim for it and . . . JUMP!

Acknowledgements

Huge thanks to Lisa.

Elyse Dodgson's family for the permission to use excerpts from *Motherland*.

Gerry Anderson and everyone at Supermarionation: your creativity inspired me as a child, when I would watch *Stingray*, *Thunderbirds*, *Captain Scarlet* and *Fireball XL5*.

Lew Grade stuff.

Man from U.N.C.L.E.-type stuff.

Top of the Pops.

Radio 1.

Blazing Saddles.

Superfly.

Shaft.

Norman Beaton.

Rudolph Walker.

Charlie Williams.

No Problem!

David Copperfield, Tracey Ullman and Paul Jackson.

Tarrant and the *Tiswas* posse.

Robert Luff.

Sidney Poitier.

Woody Strode.

The Wire.

The Sopranos.

Oz.

Breaking Bad.

Royal Holloway College.
Goldsmiths College.
The British Library.
The BFI.
Billie.
My mama.
My siblings.
Spike Lee.
Ava DuVernay.
Ryan Coogler.
Barry Jenkins.
Amma Asante.
Steve McQueen.
Meera Syal.
Sanjeev Bhaskar.
Gurinder Chadha.
Michaela Coel.
Marcus Ryder.
Pat Younge.
Angela Ferreira.
David Harewood.
Adrian Lester.
Richard Pryor.
Whoopi Goldberg.
Steve Martin.
Robin Williams.
Dudley.
Greg.
Mac.
Tom.
Mr Brookes.
Vanessa Pereira.
Sue Hunter.

Kirstie McLeod.
Richard Curtis.
Kevin Cahill.
Peter Bennett-Jones.
The McIntyre organisation.
Robin Nash.
Louis Prima.
Earth, Wind & Fire.
Cameo.
Parliament-Funkadelic.
Soul II Soul.
Mica Paris.
Bob Marley and the Wailers.
UB40.
The Average White Band.
Martyn Symonds.
The Lockshen Gang.
Lucy Robinson.
Ed Bye.

I've worked with some fabulous writers. Here's a few of them (but thanks to everyone who's ever put pen to paper with/for me):

Kim Fuller.
Tony Sarchet.
James Hendrie.
Geoff Atkinson.
Jon Canter.
Universal Grinding Wheel (Eamon, James and Martin).
Stan Hey.
Peter Tilbury.
Danny Robins.

WHO AM I, AGAIN?

Crucial Films posse.
Douglas Road posse.
Emily Rees Jones.
Rebecca Ptaszynski.